# FAITHFUL & TRUE

# FAITHFUL & TRUE

A rare photograph collection celebrating Man's Best Friend

NEW HOLLAND

# INTRODUCTION

Blackheath, in south-east London, is one of the city's most lovely green spaces. The heath, all 211 acres of it, stretches from Blackheath 'village' to the edge of Greenwich Park, its perimeter prettily trimmed with pastel-hued Georgian and Victorian houses. It is a good place to walk dogs. Pet owners traverse it daily with their charges trotting ahead excitedly, or occasionally cajoled, reluctantly, into taking their daily constitutional.

On the corner of the heath, on the edge of the village, sits a former parish hall, now the home of Mary Evans Picture Library, a 50 year-old Blackheath institution. The library, which specialises in history, has been supplying pictures of the past to a variety of publishing, media and design clients for the past five decades. Its founder, Mary, was a great dog lover herself and before her death in 2010 she could be seen each day making the most of Blackheath's bucolic charms in the company of her own canine companion, Nina, one of a succession of King Charles Spaniels she doted on.

It is no surprise therefore, that the inherent collecting bug within Mary extended to amassing a wealth of historic material on dogs, from books and scraps to photographs and postcards. Among the treasures filling what became known as 'Mary's dog room' in her Blackheath home, were several albums filled with photographs taken of people with their dogs.

The pictures date from the late 19th century (when dog ownership reached cult status, spearheaded by Queen Victoria herself) up to the middle of the 20th century. They vary from the simple snapshot to formal studio portraits, made less so by the inclusion of a characterful family pet, brought along in order to be captured for posterity with their owners. Sometimes in these pictures, the dog is centre stage, such as a perky Manchester Terrier perched on a pedestal. At other times, they are casual, or incidental bystanders, perhaps snoozing on the lawn of an Edwardian garden, but always, they are very much part of the fabric of everyday life.

There are pictures of babies and children with dogs; men, women, servants and soldiers – while breeds vary from sharp, agile sheepdogs to pampered Pekingese or Pomeranians to the most endearing sort of Heinz 57. Whatever the breed of the dog or the kind of owner, the pictures form a moving record of how dogs have become not only beloved pets but honorary family members through each generation.

These simple and personal mementoes of the bond between owner and pet seem to show our forebears at their most tender, sincere and relaxed. Despite the starched collars and corseted bearing, these are people just like you or I; caring compassionate, jolly or joking. The presence of a dog in an old photograph makes the past suddenly familiar, and gives the sitter personality and life. More than anything, they are a reminder that, through the decades, dogs have perennially offered us undivided loyalty and unconditional love. Selected from the albums at Mary Evans, this is a treasury that offers a charming and moving testament to the value of these most faithful and true of friends.

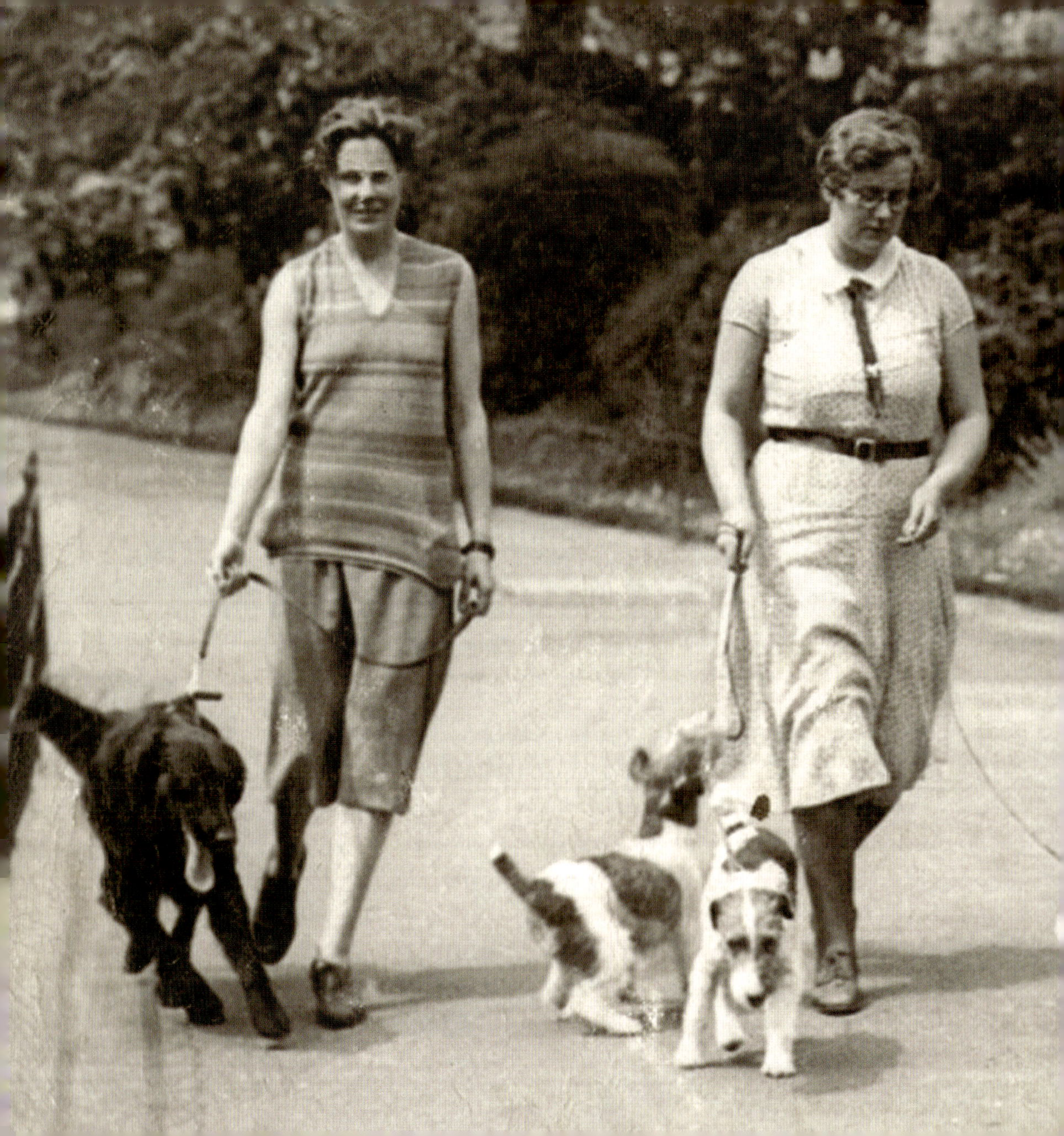

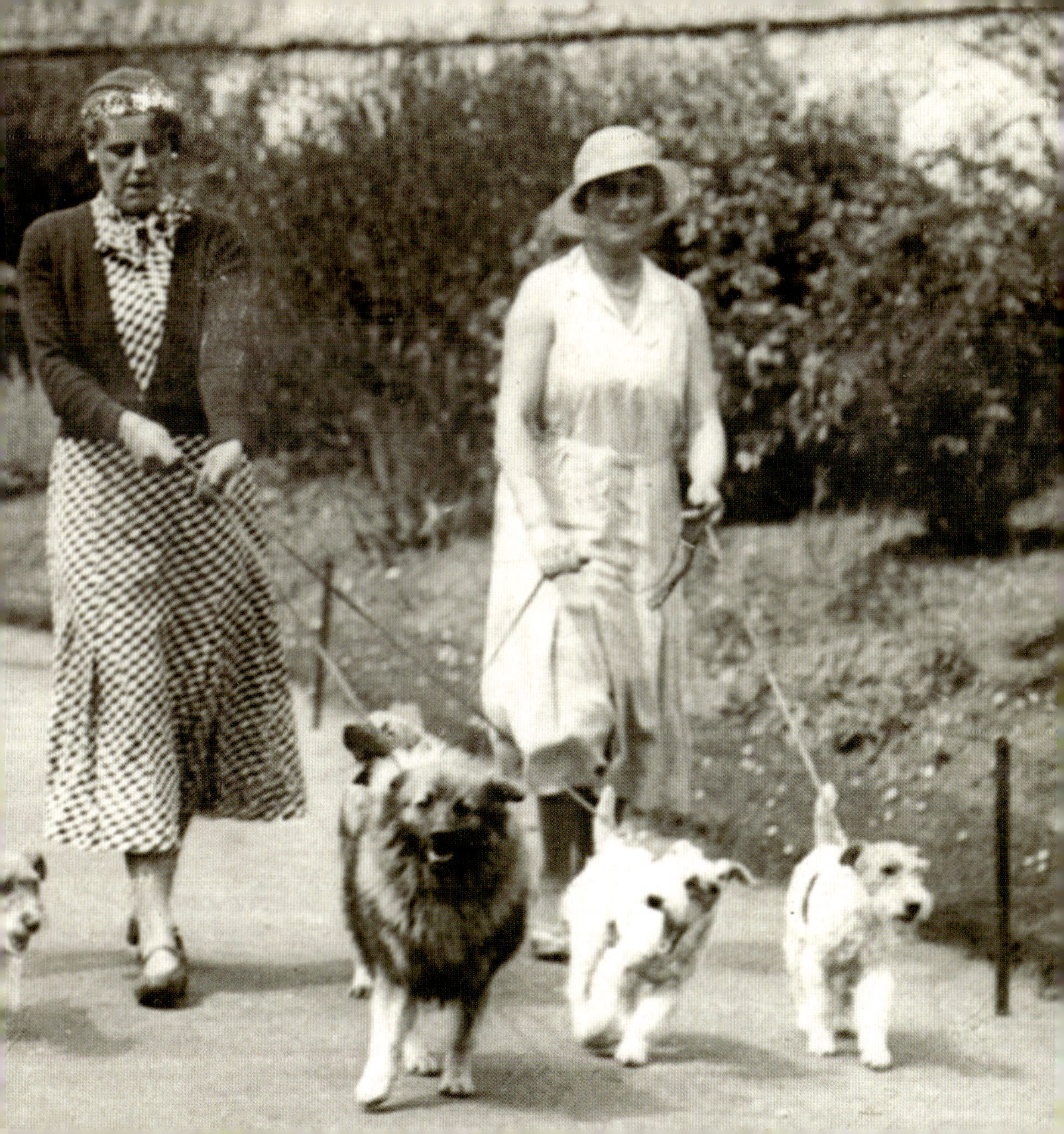

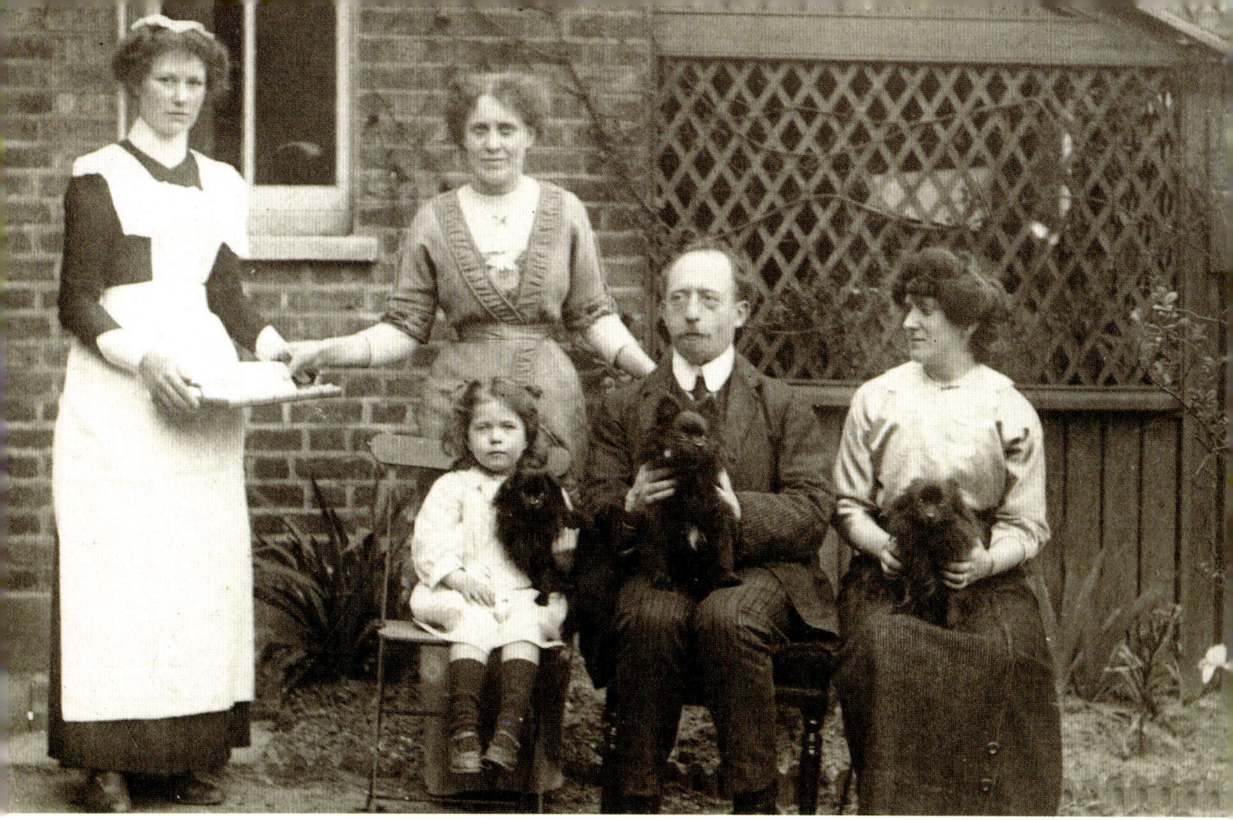

Dogs are not our whole life, but they make our lives whole.

*Roger Caras, photographer and writer*

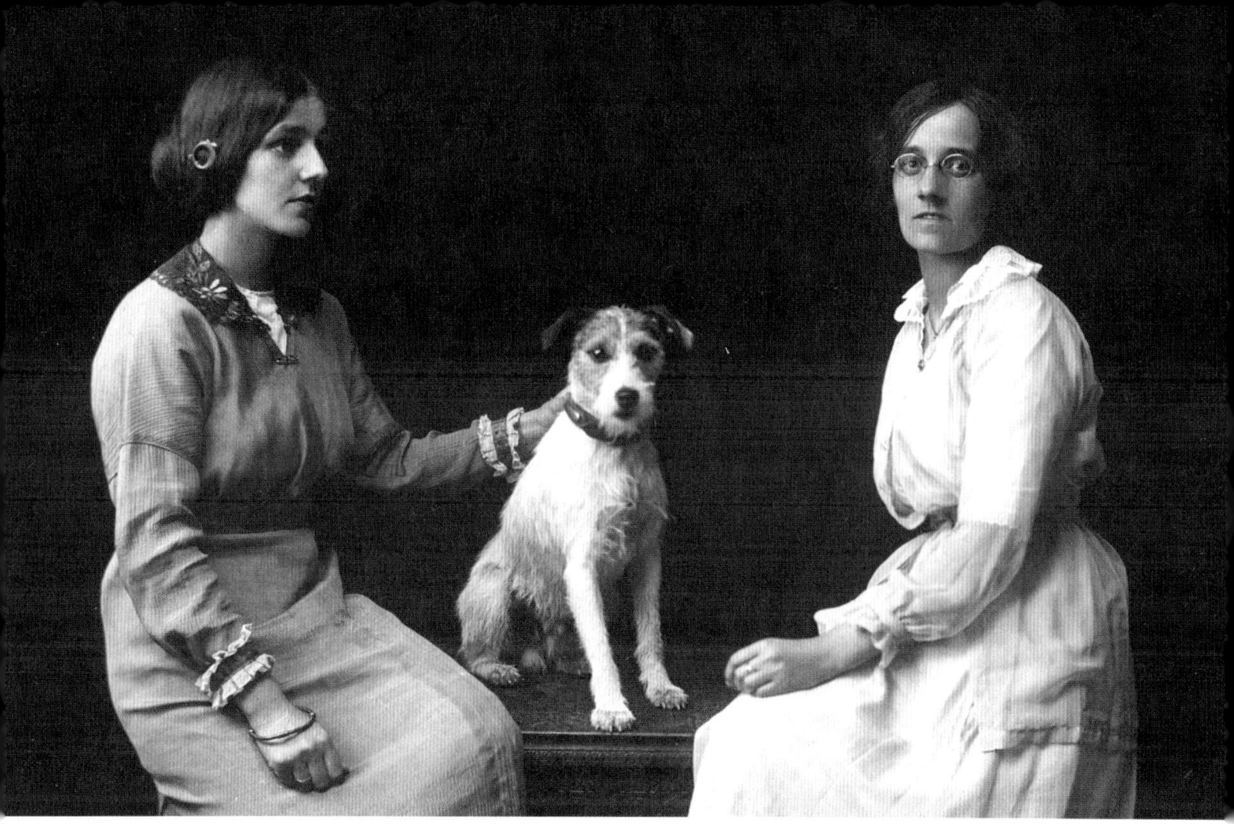

A dog is the only thing on earth that loves you more than you love yourself.

*Josh Billings, author*

He clothes himself in a sovereign grace and elegance, he makes himself smaller than a doll to sleep on our knees by the fireside, or even consents, should our fancy demand it, to appear a little ridiculous to please us.

*My Dog by Maurice Maeterlinck, illustrated by Cecil Aldin, published by George Allen & Company Ltd. 1913*

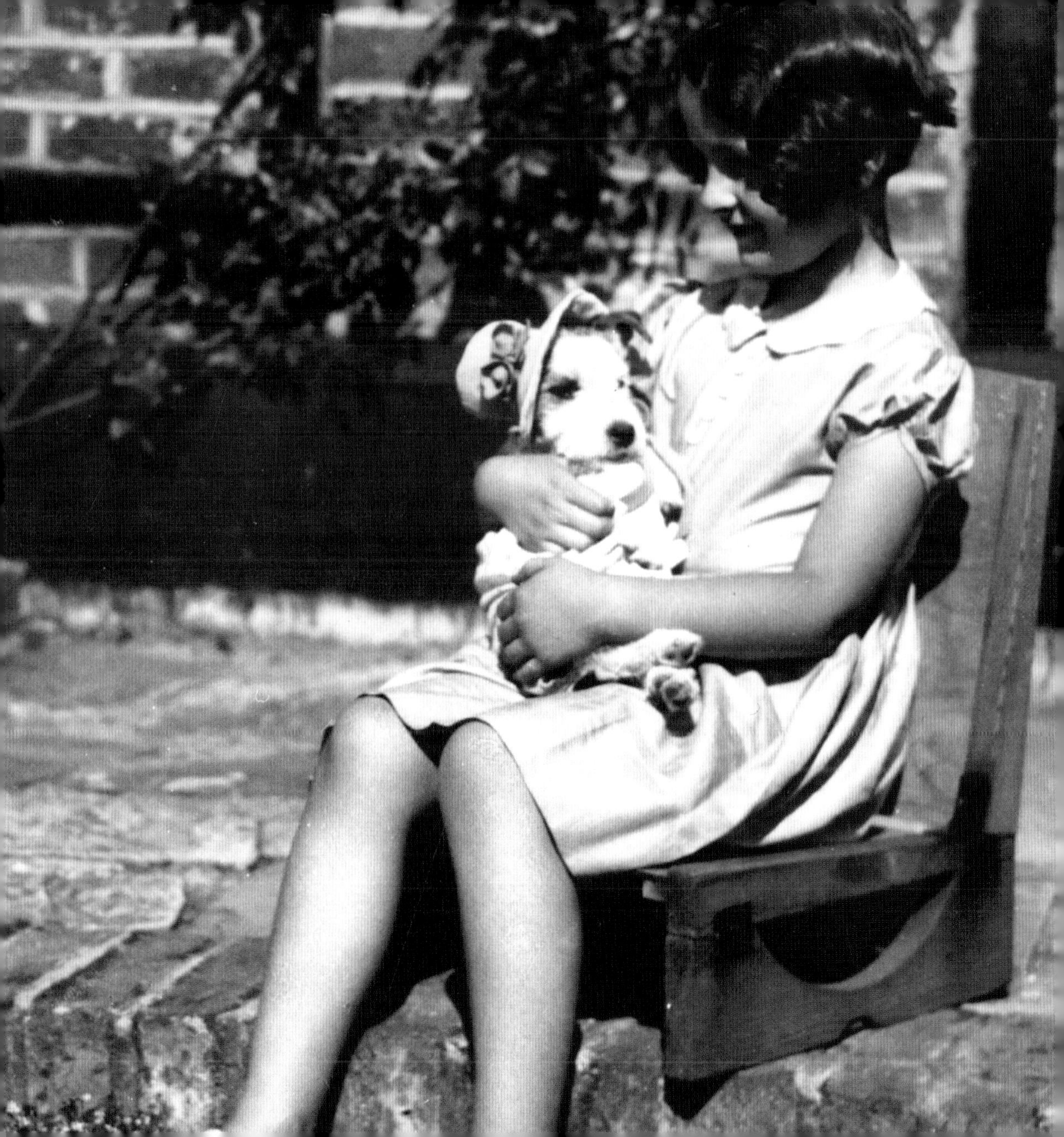

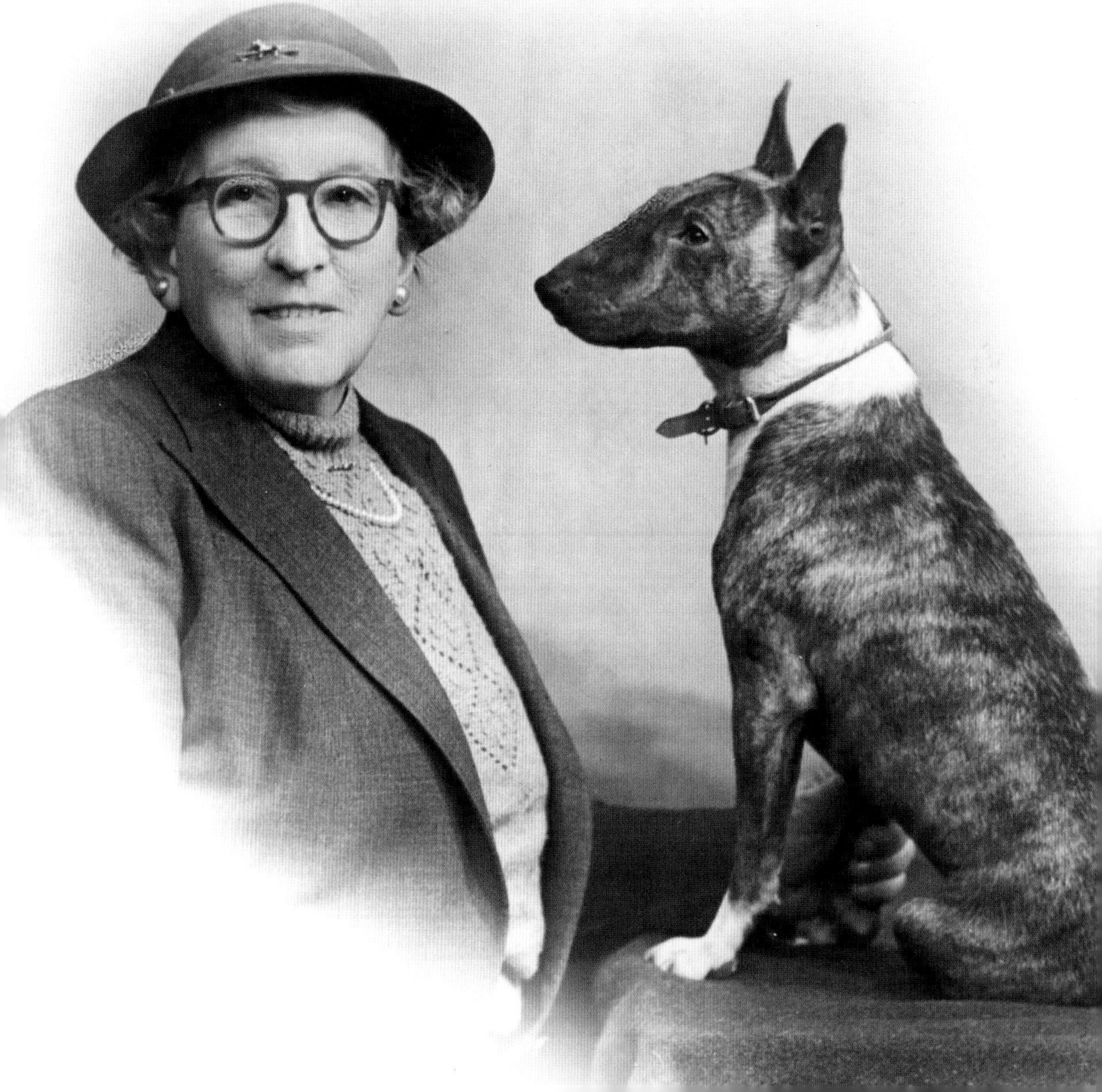

Don’t accept your dog’s admiration as conclusive evidence that you are wonderful.

*Ann Landers, advice columnist*

He is your friend, your partner, your defender,
your dog. You are his life, his love, his leader.
He will be yours, faithful and true, to the last
beat of his heart.
You owe it to him to be worthy of such devotion.

*Anon*

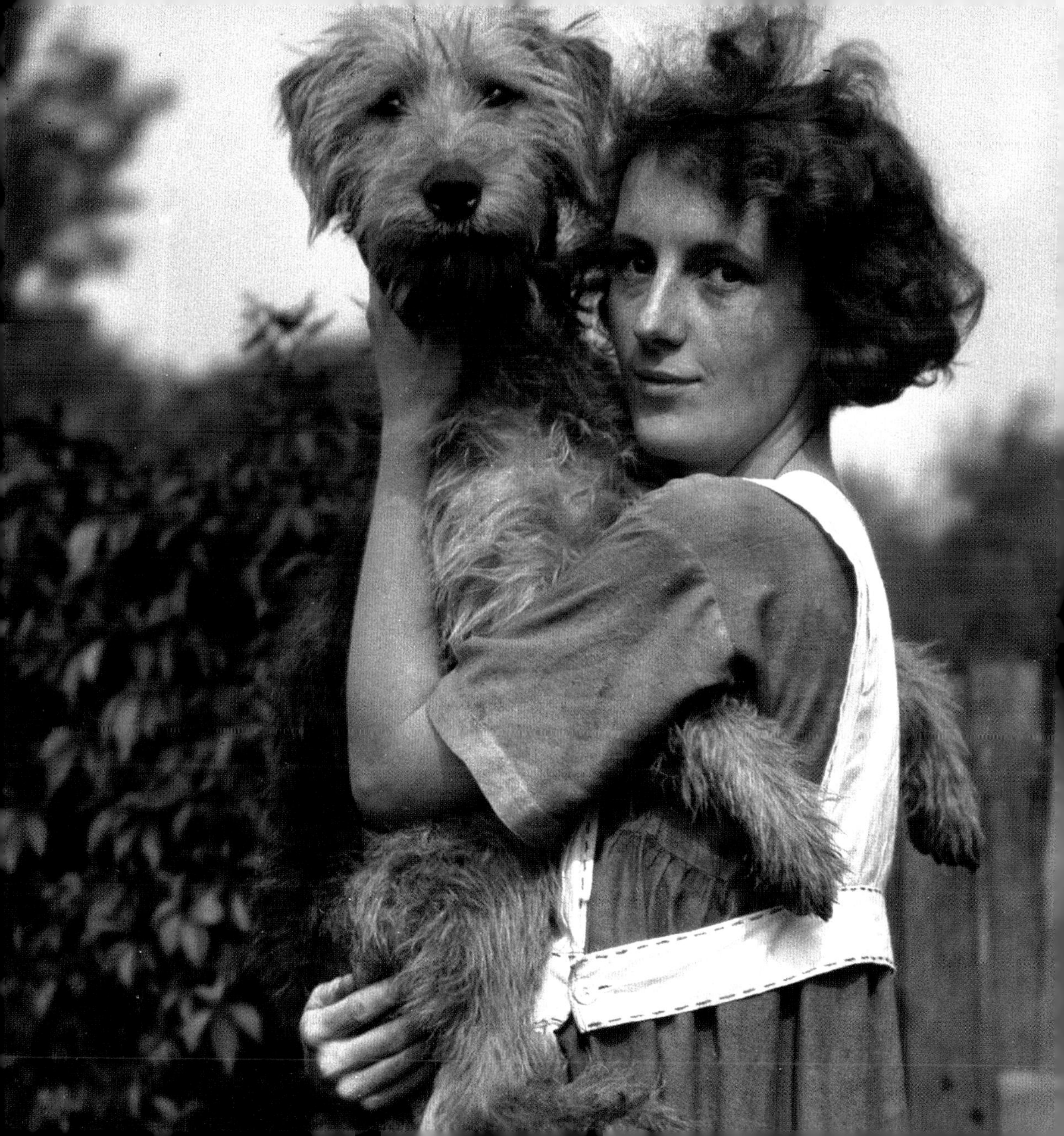

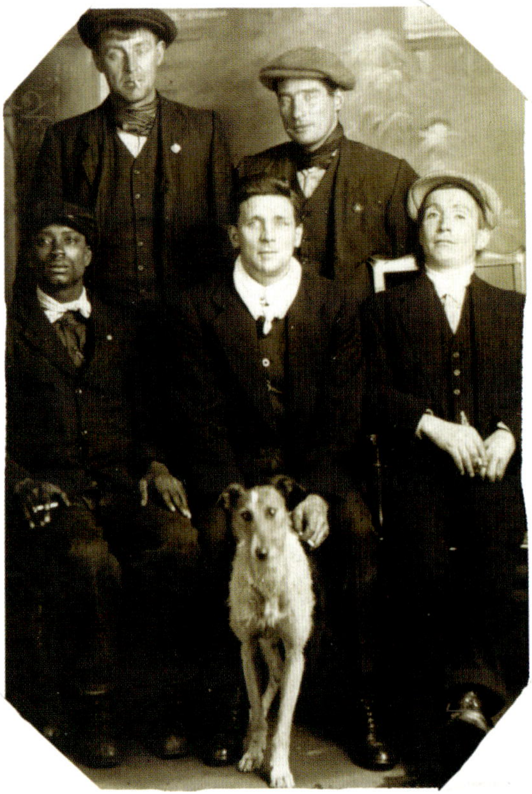

The better I know men, the more I admire dogs.

*Anon*

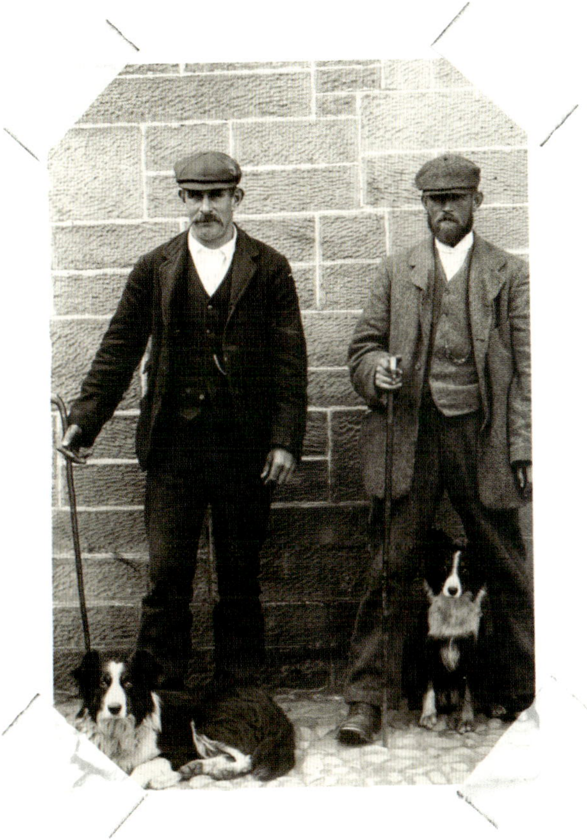

In order to really enjoy a dog, one doesn't merely try to train him to be semi-human. The point of it is to open oneself to the possibility of becoming partly a dog.

*Edward Hoagland, nature and travel writer*

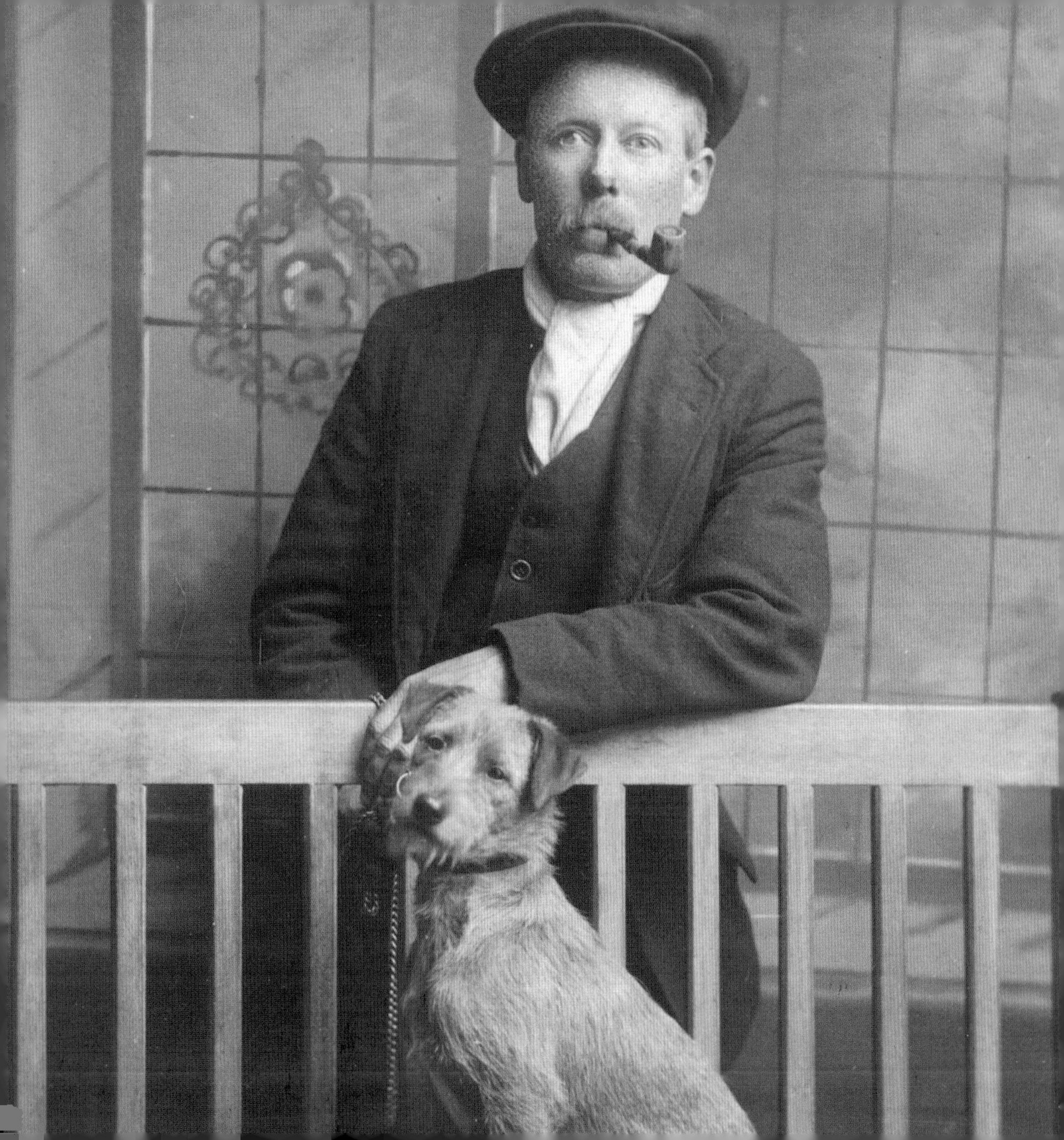

We have not to gain his confidence or his friendship: he is born our friend; while his eyes are still closed, already he believes in us: even before his birth, he has given himself to man. But the word 'friend' does not exactly depict his affectionate worship. He loves us and reveres us as though we had drawn him out of nothing.

*My Dog by Maurice Maeterlinck,*

*illustrated by Cecil Aldin,*

*published by George Allen & Company Ltd. 1913*

---

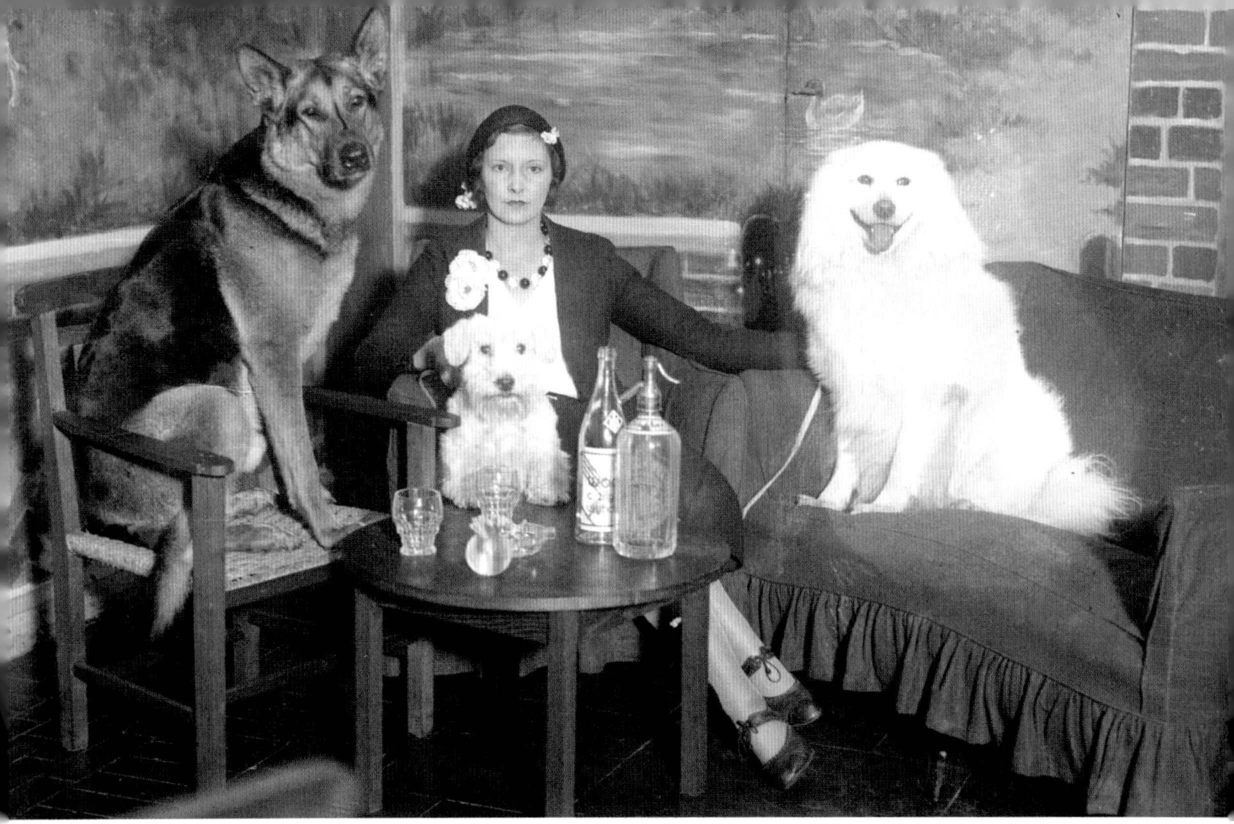

There are three faithful friends: an old wife, an old dog, and ready money.

*Benjamin Franklin, author, scientist, inventor and statesman*

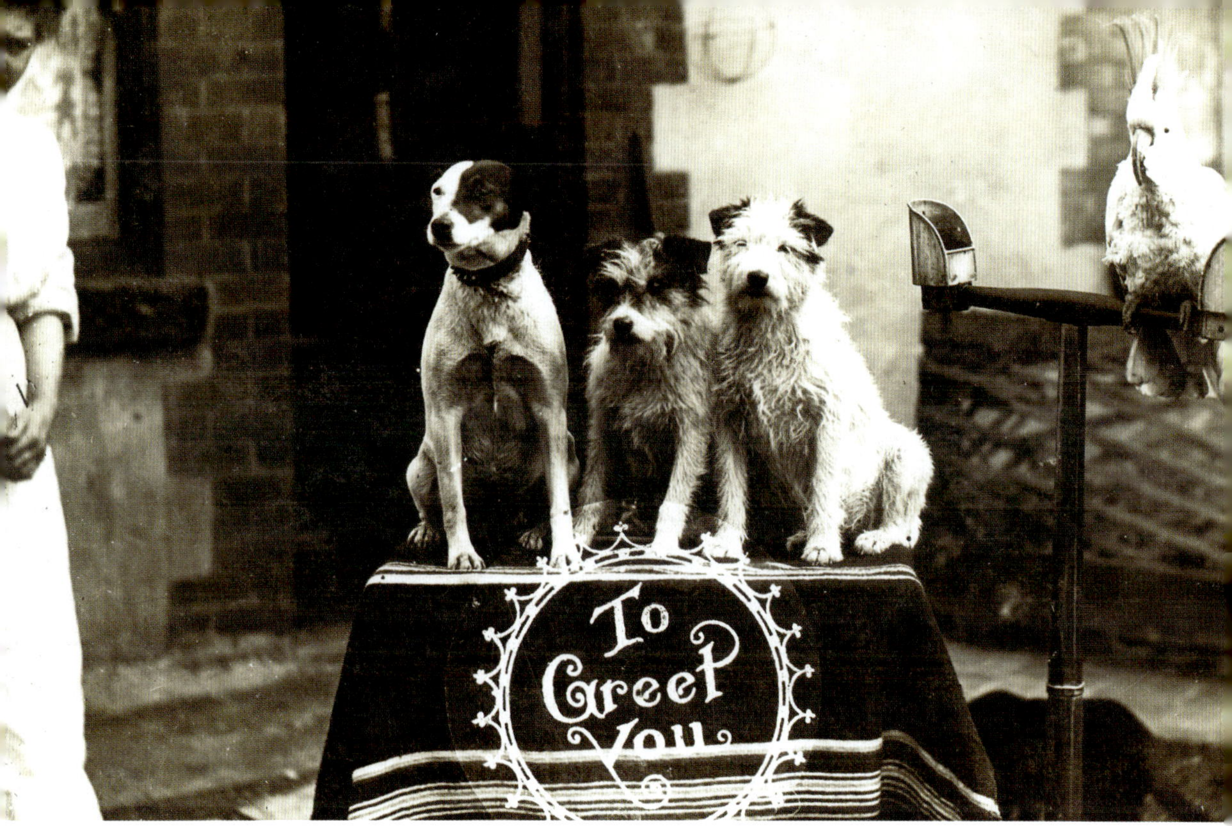


Let Hercules himself do what he may,
The cat will mew and dog will have his day.

*William Shakespeare, Hamlet*

The great pleasure of a dog is that you may make a fool of yourself with him and not only will he not scold you, but he will make a fool of himself too.

*Samuel Butler, novelist*

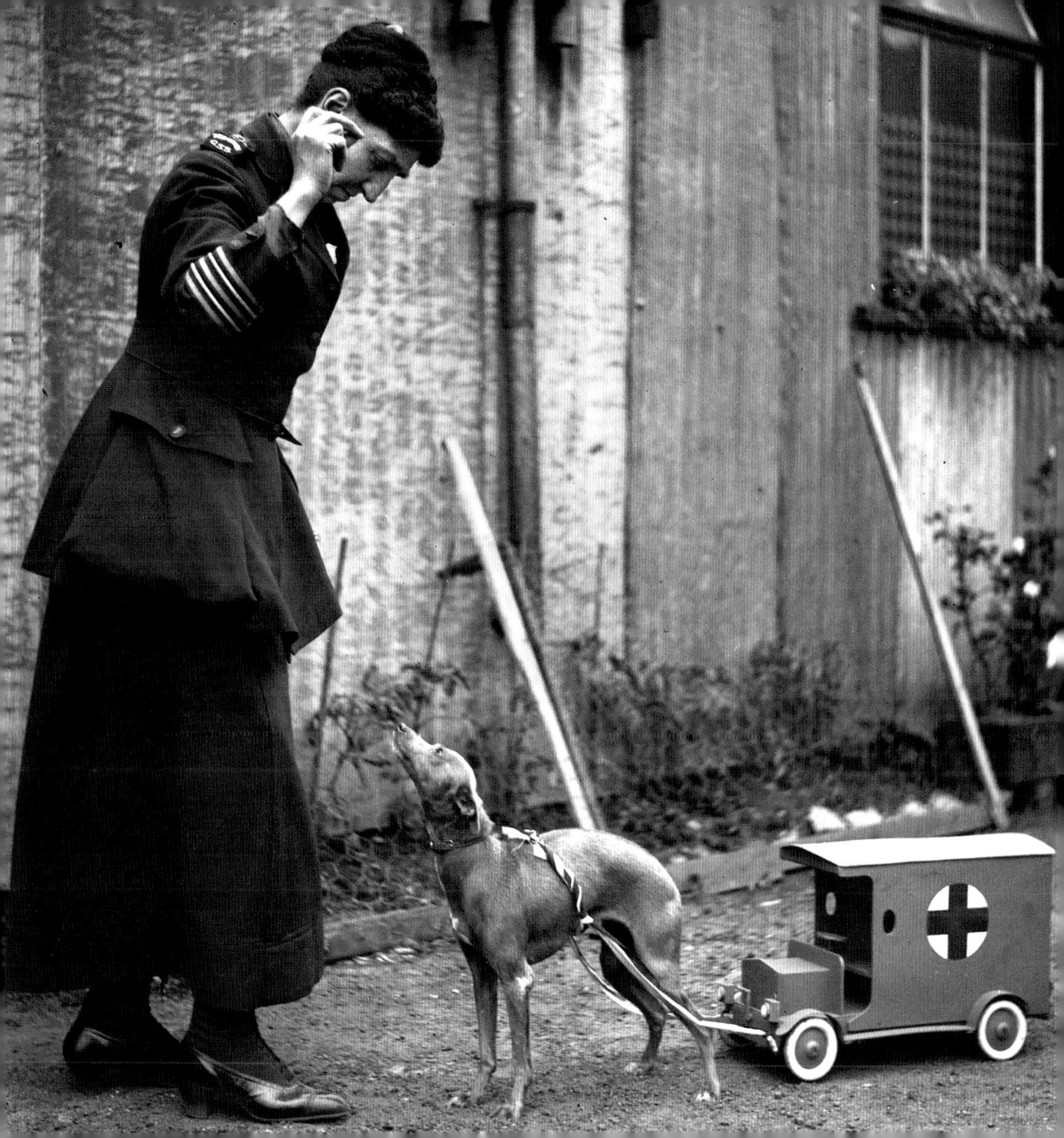

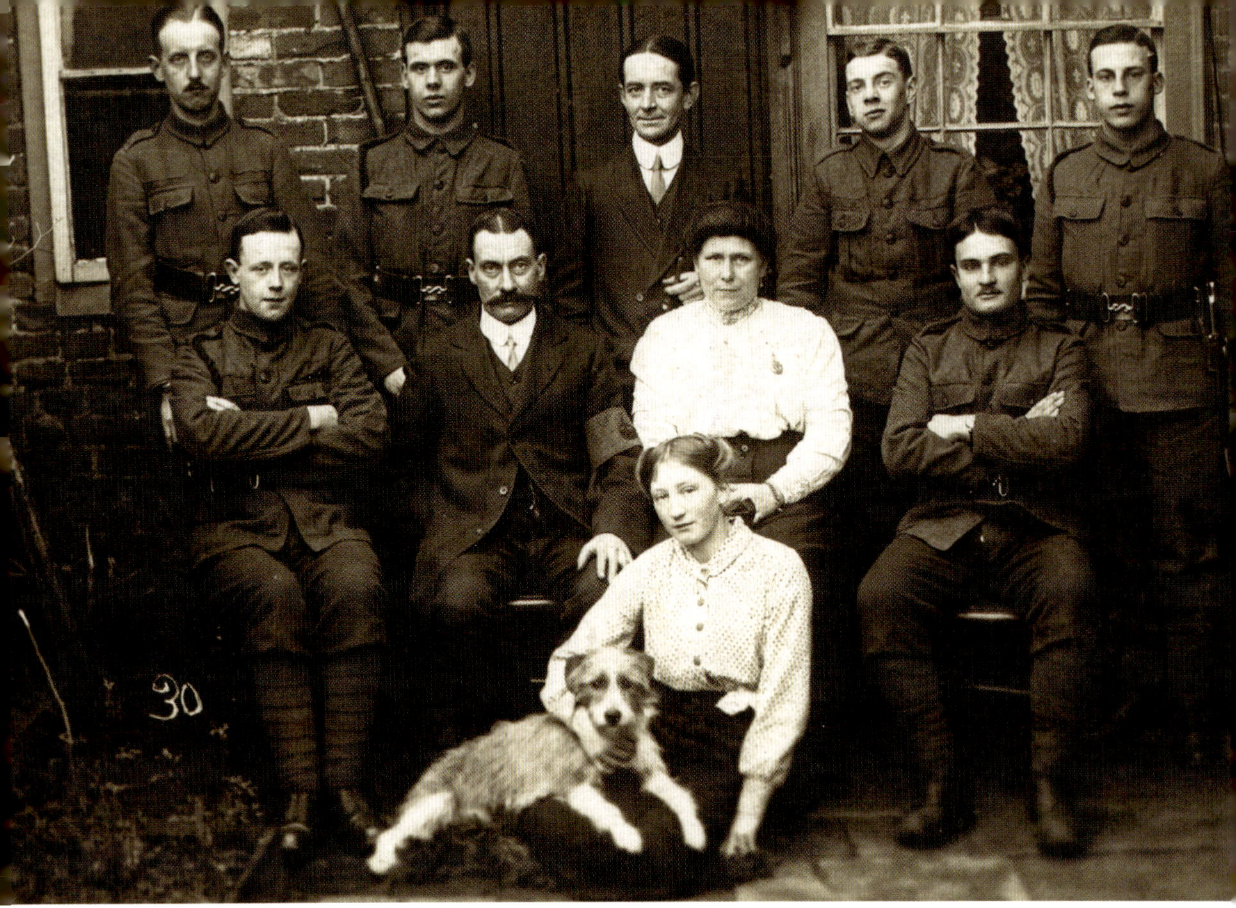


The faithful dog, the natural friend of man, Watched round his bed at sleep's unguarded hour. In deeds of death and danger led the way, And bled unconquered in the doubtful fray. With nice discriminating nose, inhales, The passing odours in the tainted gales; And clamorous Barks and points his listening ears, Bristles his wavy back, and fierce defiance growls.

*'Canine gratitude' by Joseph Taylor, 1806*

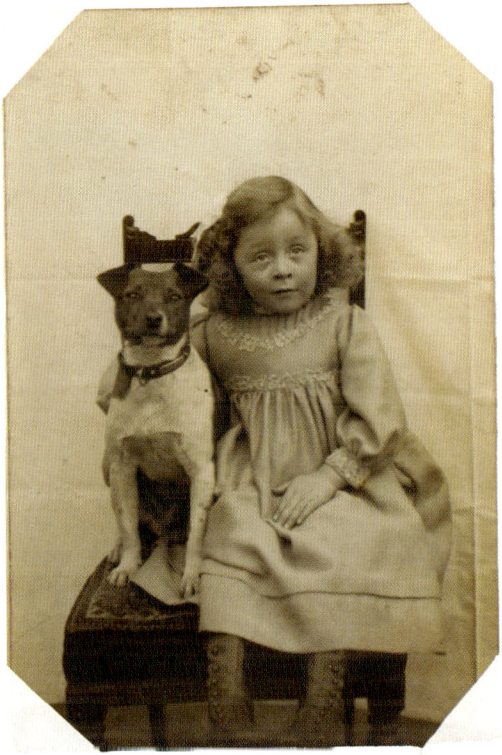

I am called a dog because I fawn on those who give me anything,
I yelp at those who refuse, and I set my teeth in rascals.

*Diogenes, Greek philosopher*

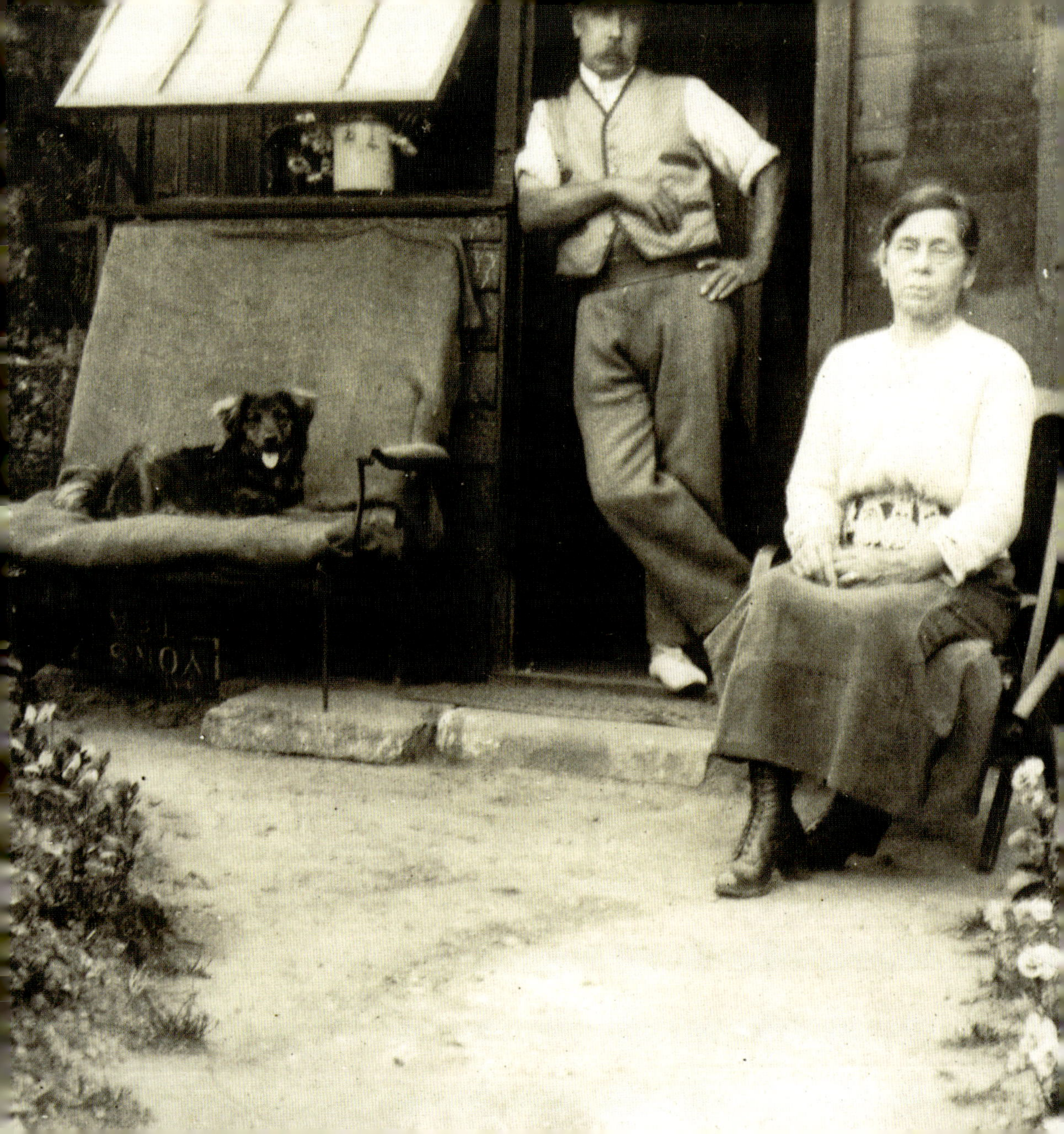

Dog. A kind of additional or subsidiary Deity designed to catch the overflow and surplus of the world's worship.

*Ambrose Bierce, journalist and short story writer*

If it wasn't for dogs, some people would never go for a walk.

*Anon*

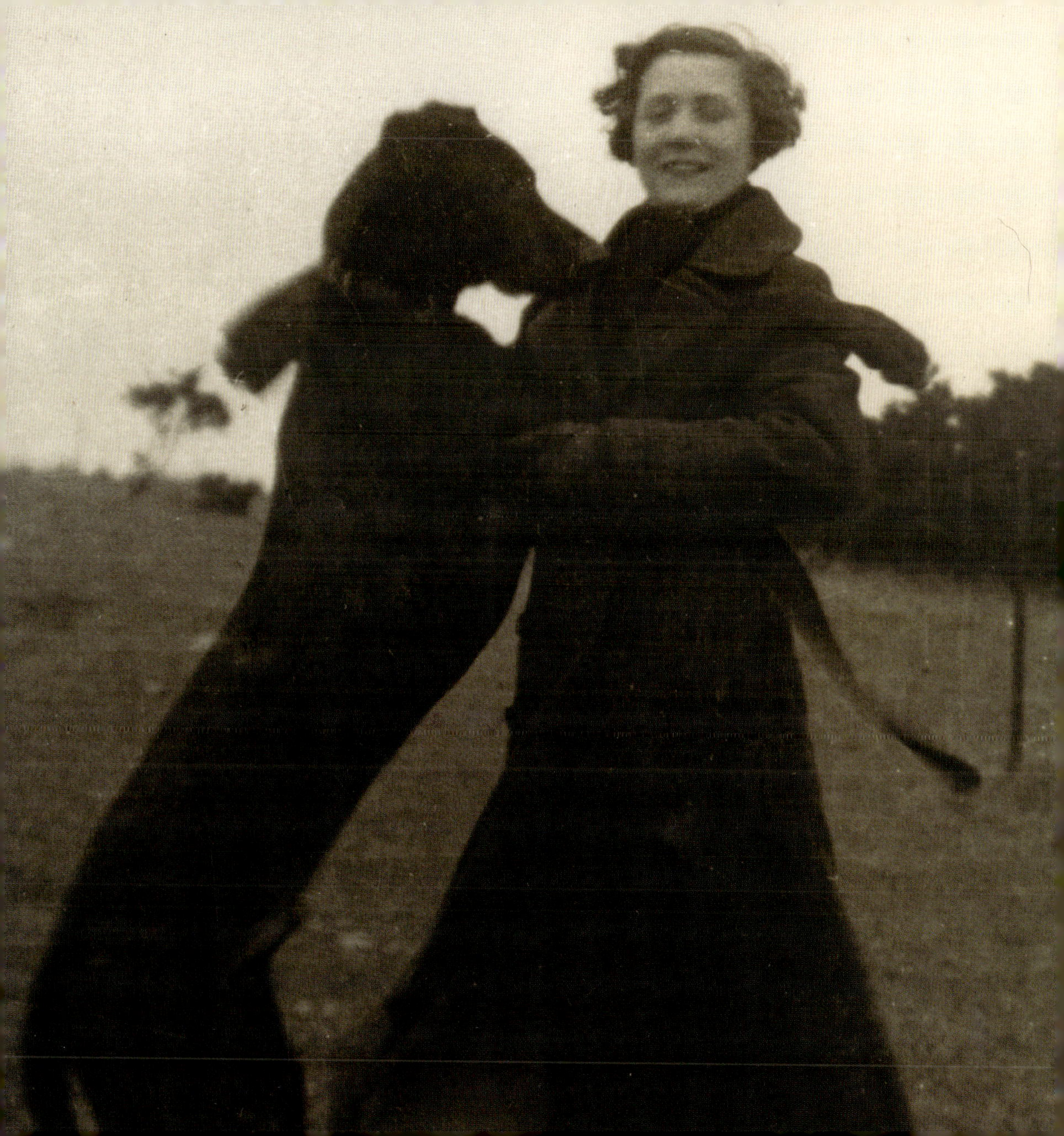

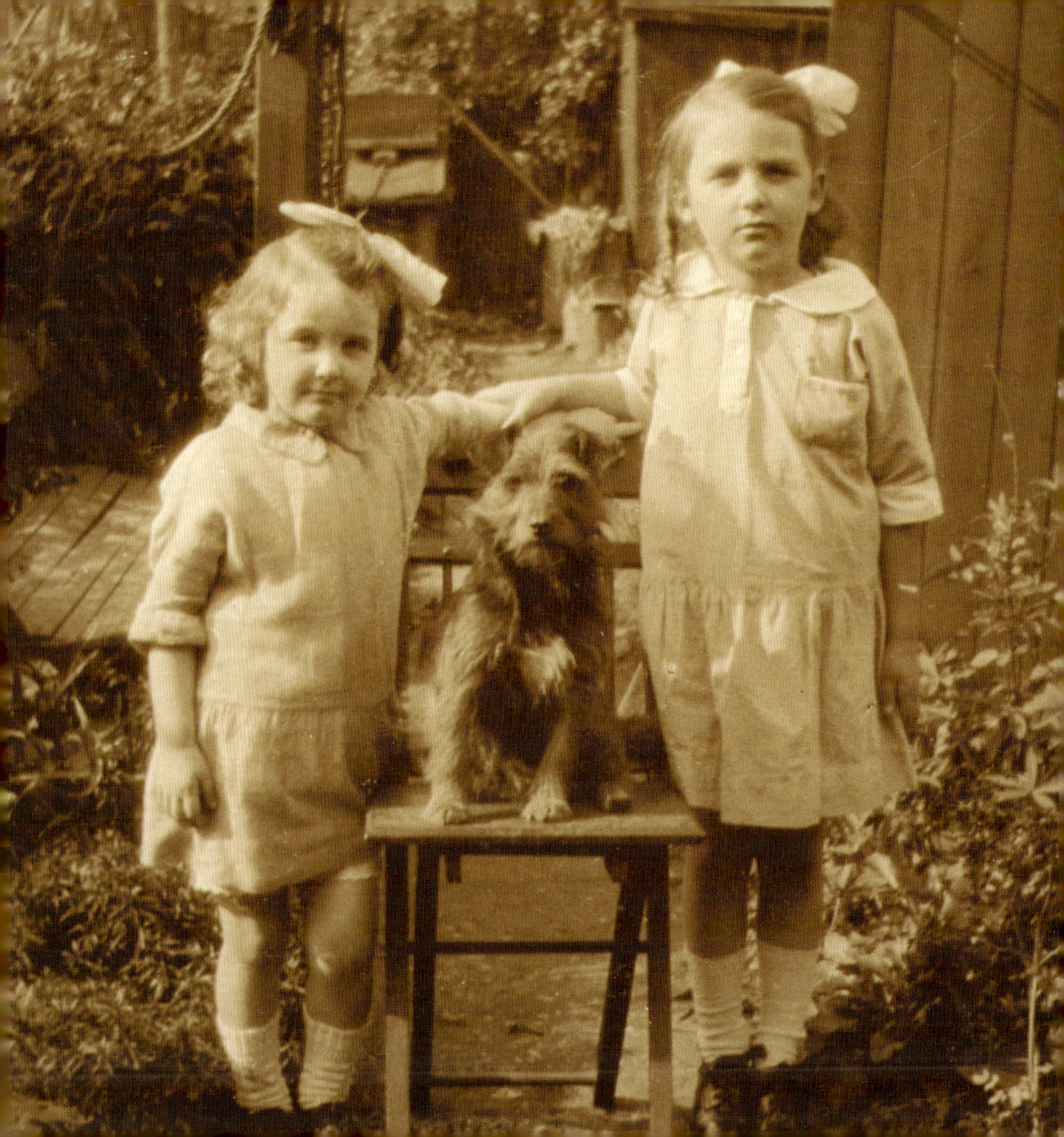

The dog barks backward without getting up.
I can remember when he was a pup.

*Robert Frost, poet*

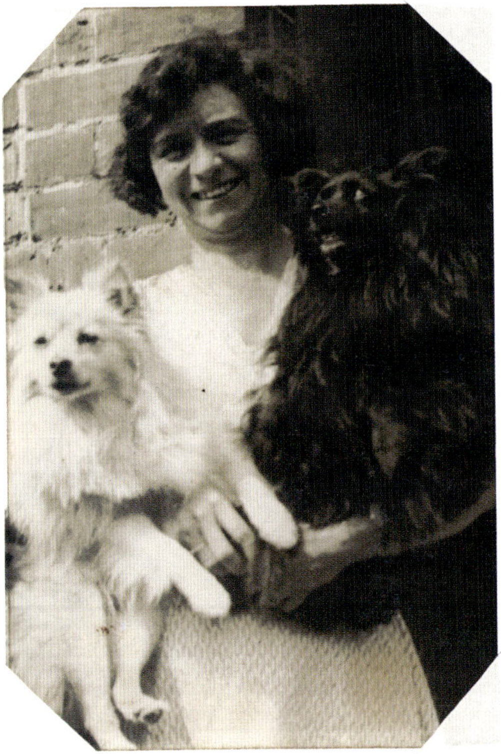

Happiness to a dog is
what lies on the other
side of a door.

*Charlton Ogburn Jr.,*
*journalist and author*

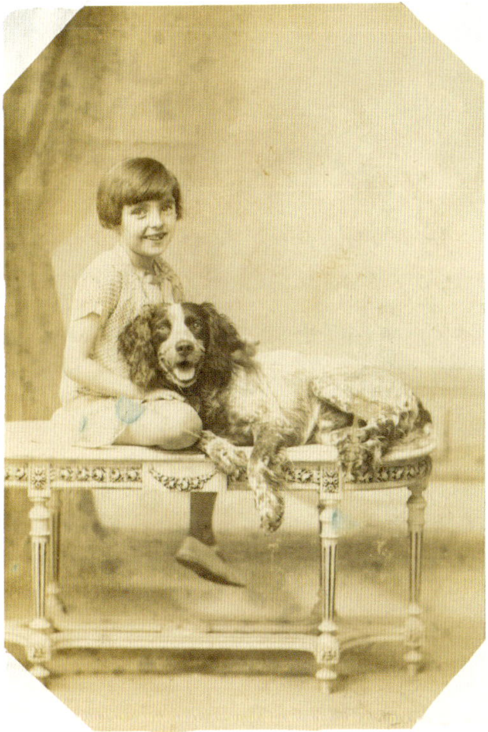

(When asked who her companions were): Hills, sir, and the sundown, and a dog as large as myself that my father bought me. They are better than human beings, because they know but do not tell.

*Emily Dickinson, poet*

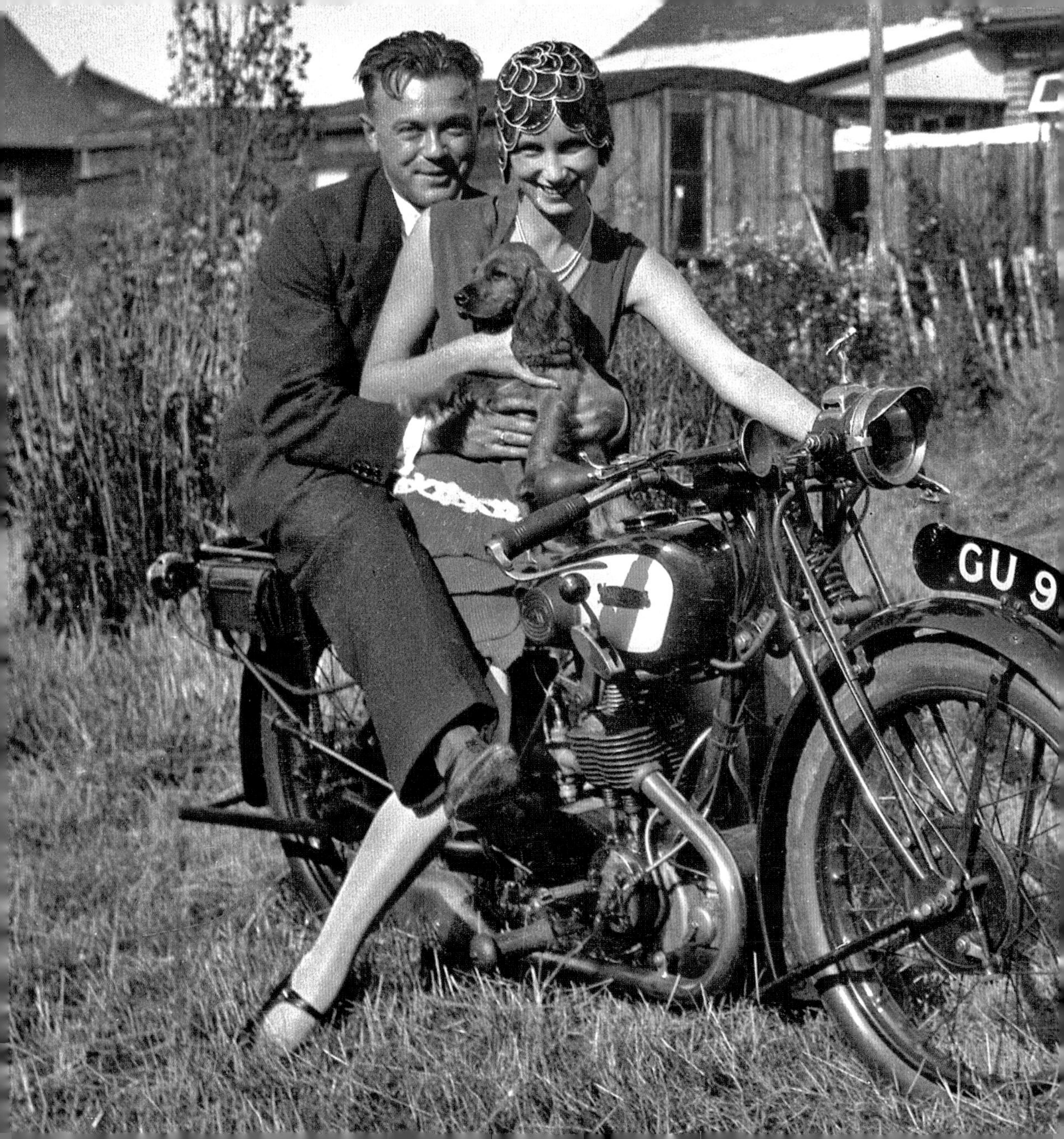
GU 9

Buy a pup and
your money will buy
love unflinching.

*Rudyard Kipling, author and poet*

In man, true friendship I long strove to find
But missed my aim;
At length I found it in my dog most kind.
Man! blush for shame.

*Joseph Taylor, published in Canine Gratitude (1806)*

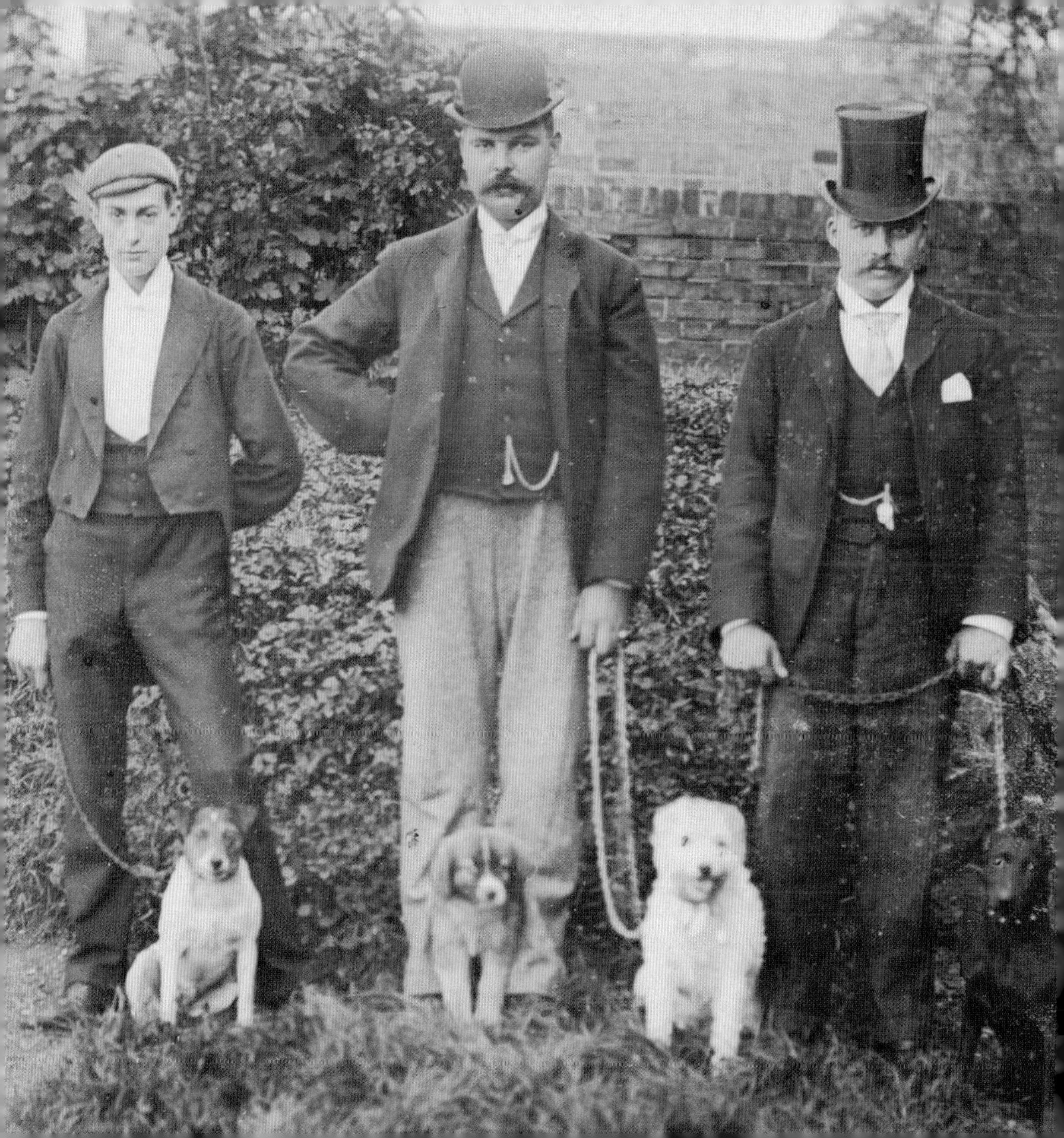

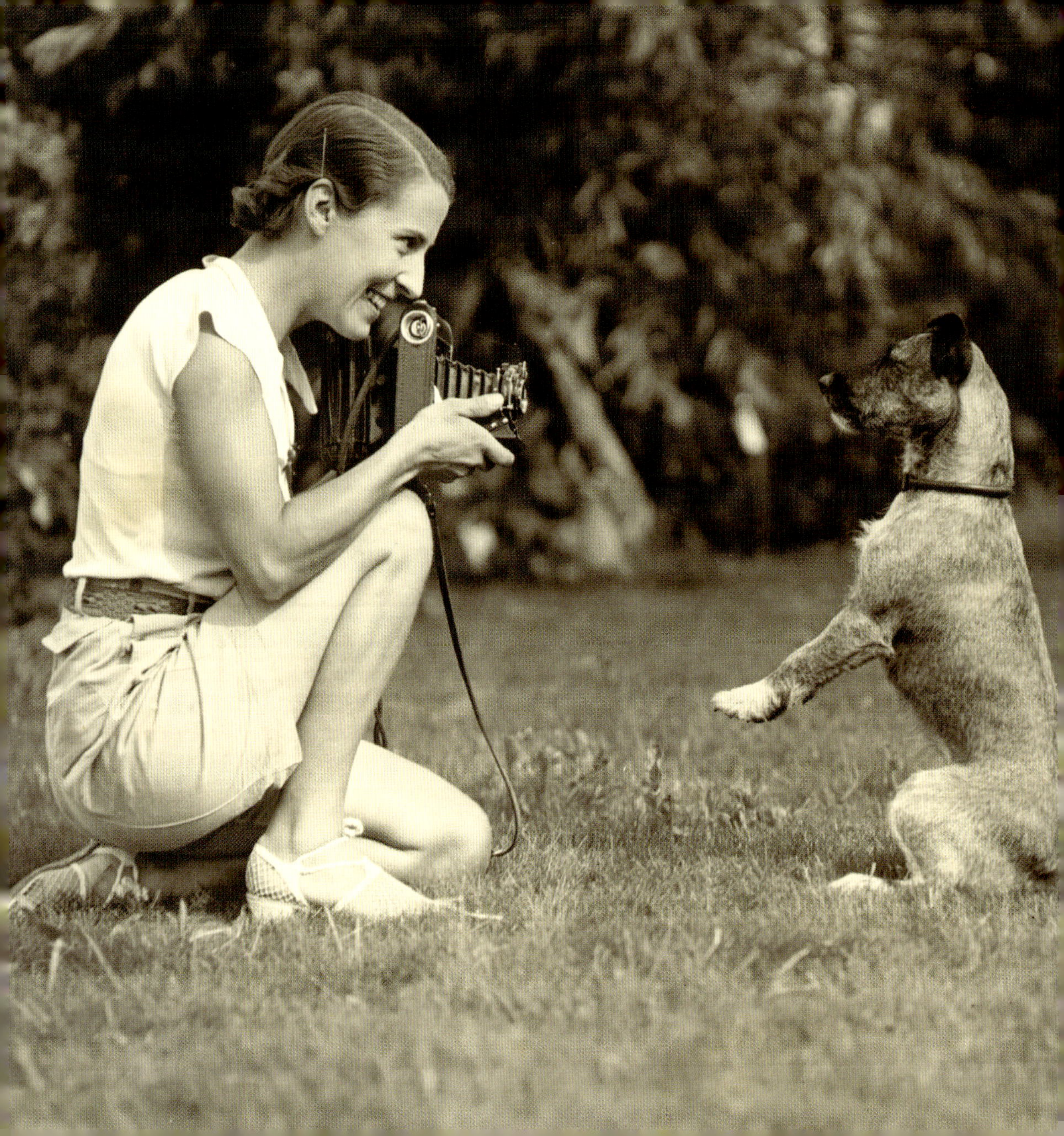

Pray steal me not, I'm Mrs. Dingley's,
Whose heart in this four-footed thing lies.

*On the collar of Mrs Dinglsy's lapdog by Jonathan Swift, satirist and poet. Works of the British Poets, 1828.*

---

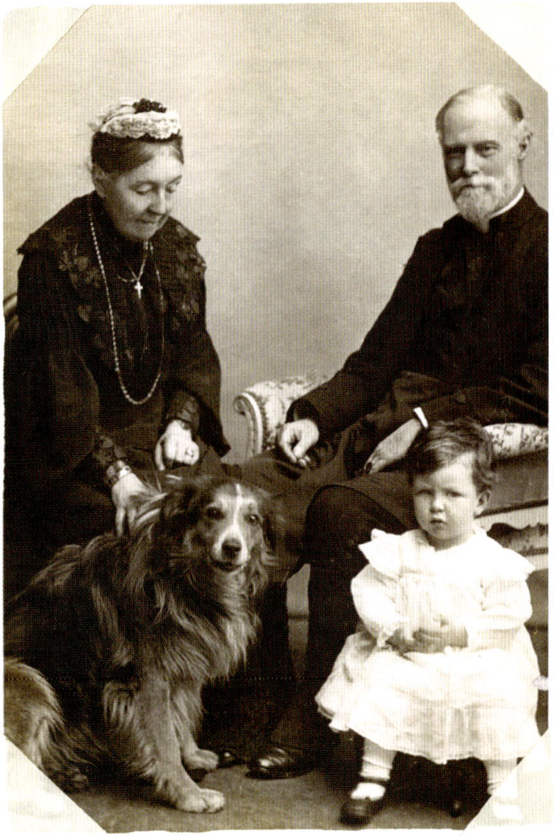

No one appreciates the very special genius of your conversation as the dog does.

*Christopher Morley*

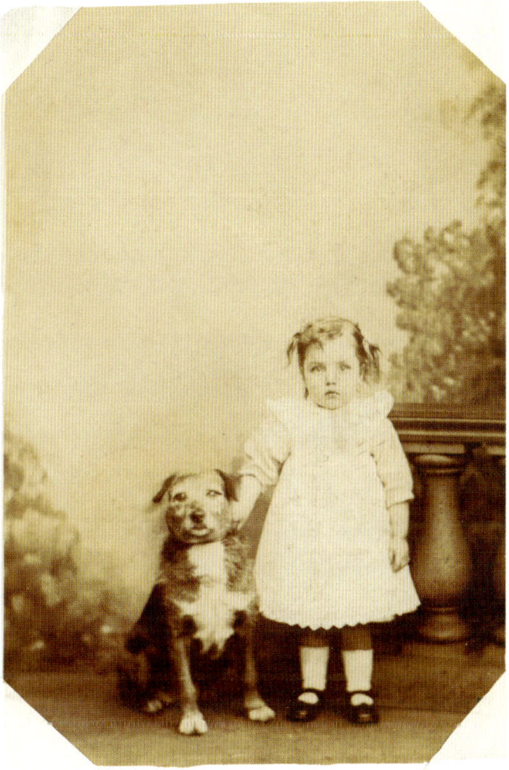

The psychological and moral comfort of a presence at once humble and understanding—this is the greatest benefit that the dog has bestowed upon man.

*Percy Bysshe Shelley, poet*

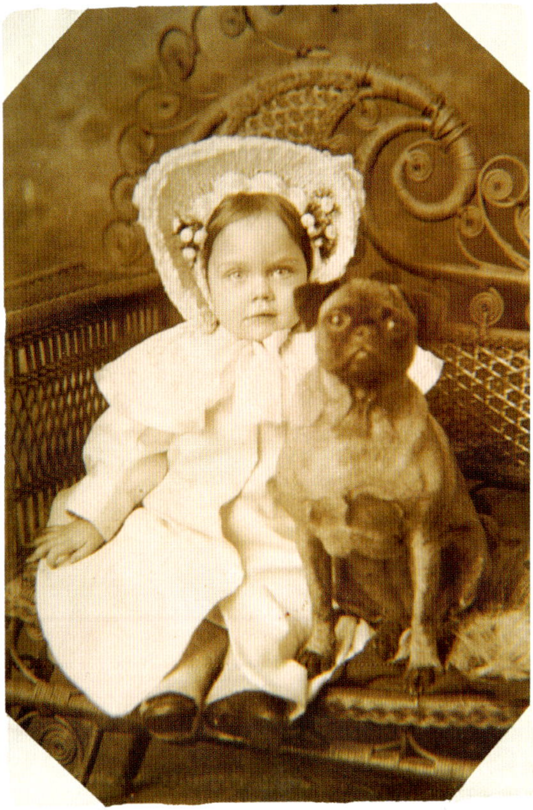

My pug makes a bad pet; he is useless in the field, is somewhat snappish, has little sagacity, and is very cowardly; but there is an air of bon ton about him which renders him a fashionable appendage to a fine lady.

*Parisian gossip, 19th century*

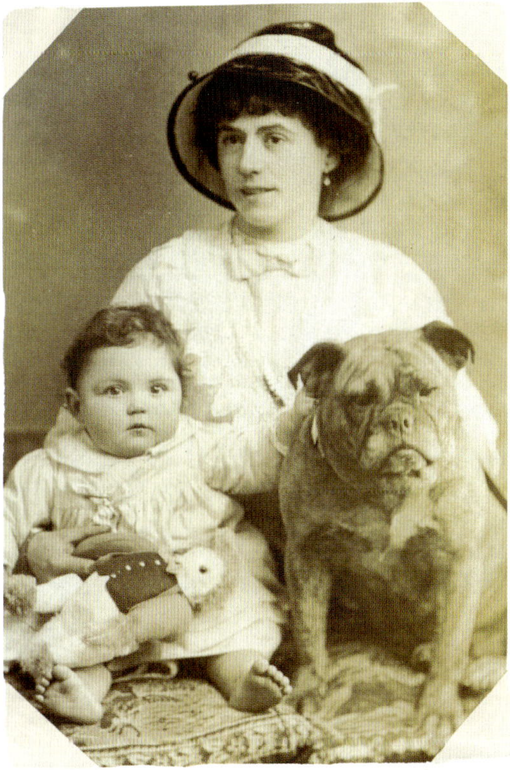

The nose of the bulldog has been slanted backwards so that he can breathe without letting go.

*Winston Churchill,*
*statesman and author*

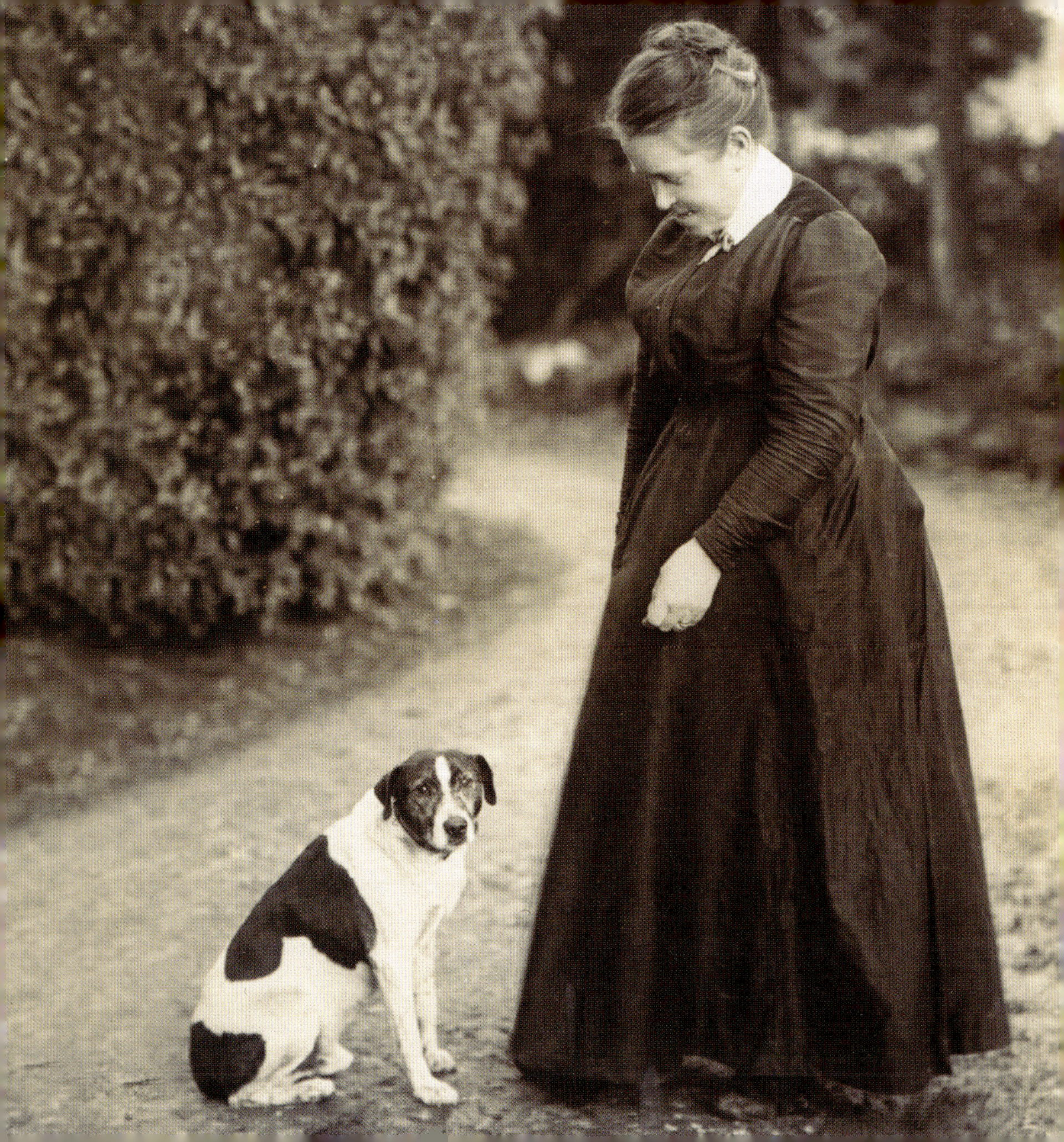

Half an hour a day – while you smoke the after breakfast pipe – devoted to the education of your puppy, ought in, say three months, to ground him pretty well in retrieving in proper form – dropping and staying, and coming to whistle.

*From 'Breaking and Training Dogs'*

*by Pathfinder and Hugh Dalziel (1885)*

I am his Highness dog at Kew; pray tell me, sir, whose dog are you?

*Alexander Pope, poet*

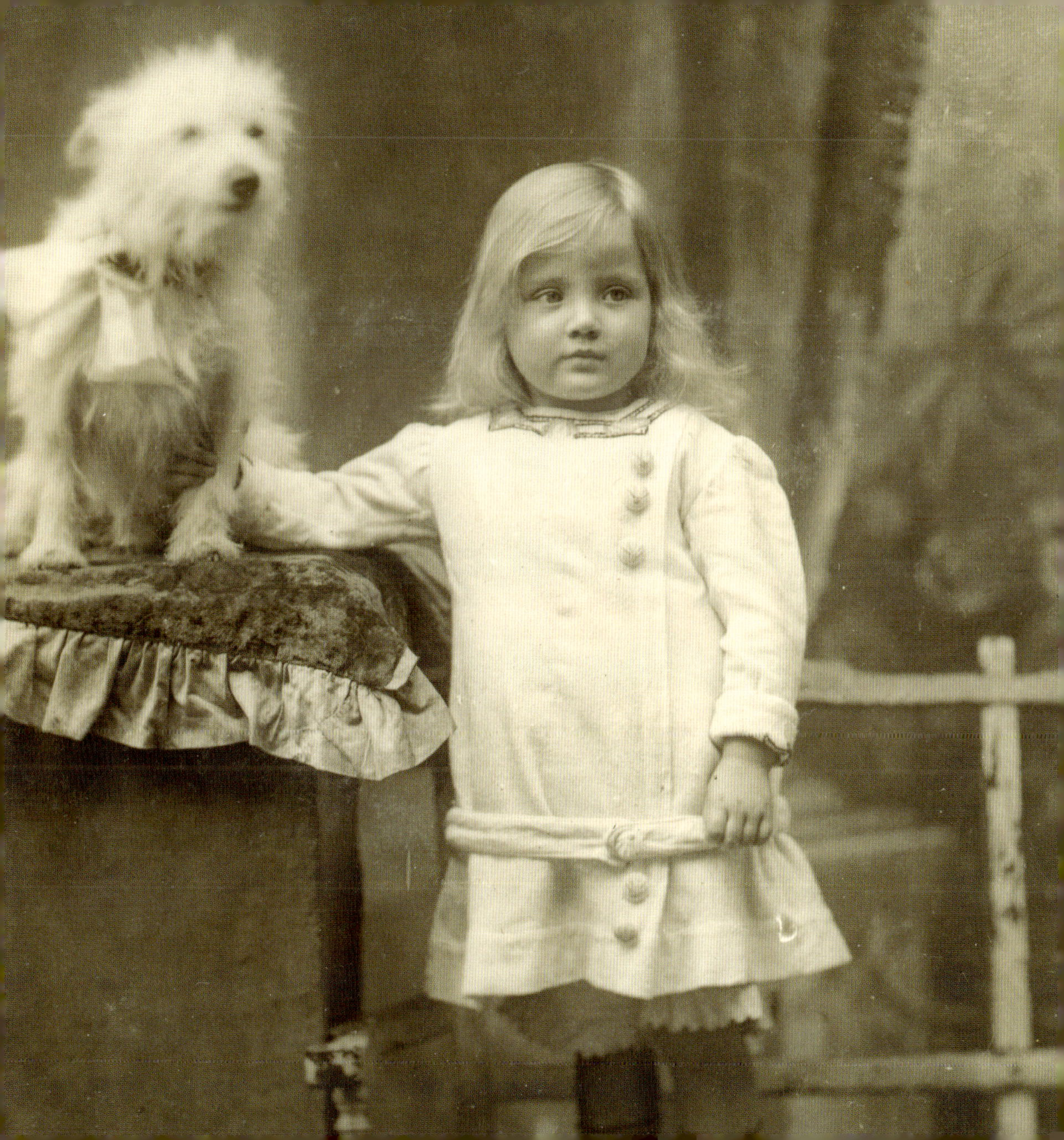

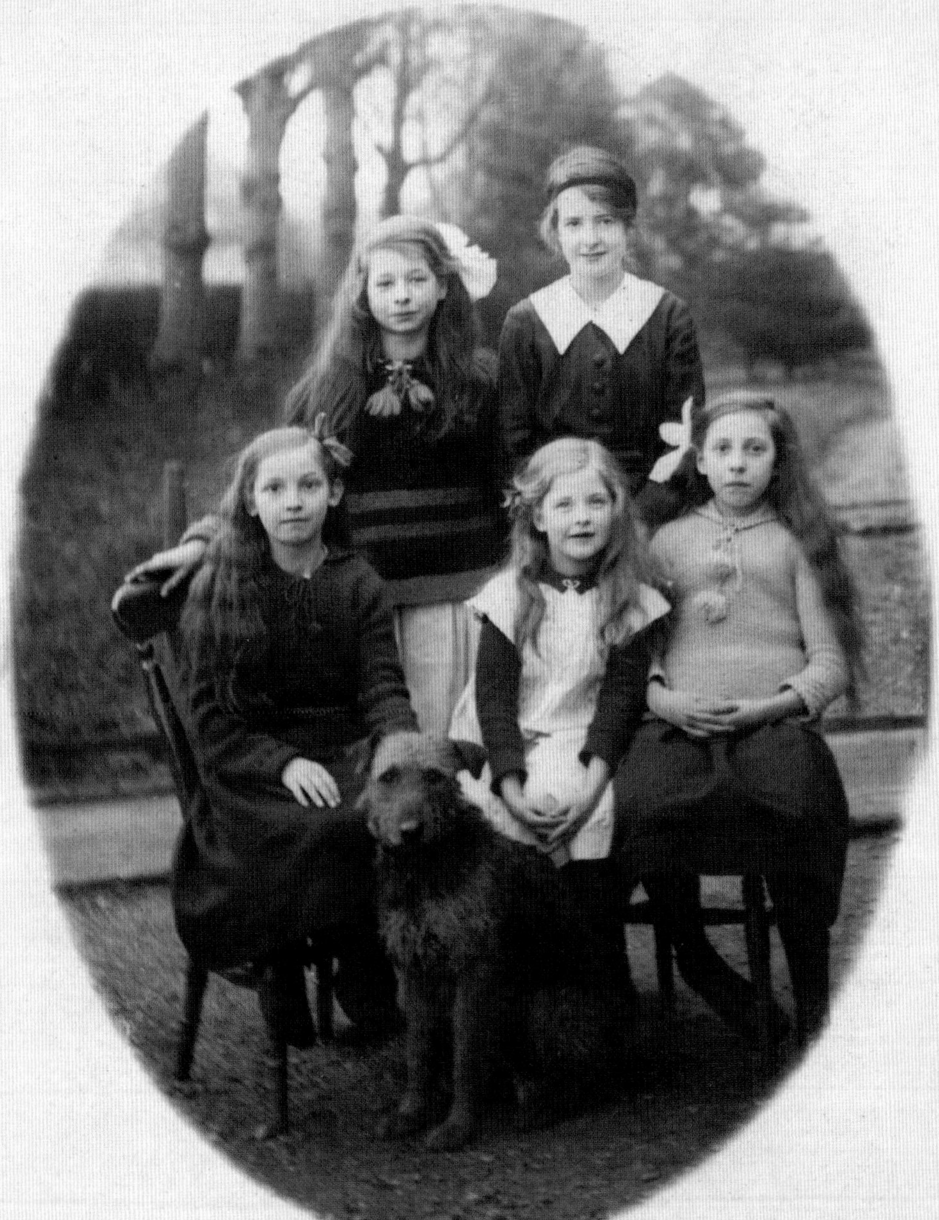

If we wish to be really kind to a "dumb" creature whom we have attached to ourselves, so that we say "my dog," or "my cat," with a special sense of ownership or mastery, to begin by trying to become familiar with it, so as to understand, as far as may be, what gives it pleasure or pain, and how much we have a right to expect of it in the way of friendship or service; in both cases we shall probably find that we receive not "what we give," but something far beyond it.

*From Domestic Pets:*

*Their Habits and Treatments*

*by C. Pridham (c.1890)*

Happiness is a warm puppy.

*Charles M. Schulz, cartoonist*

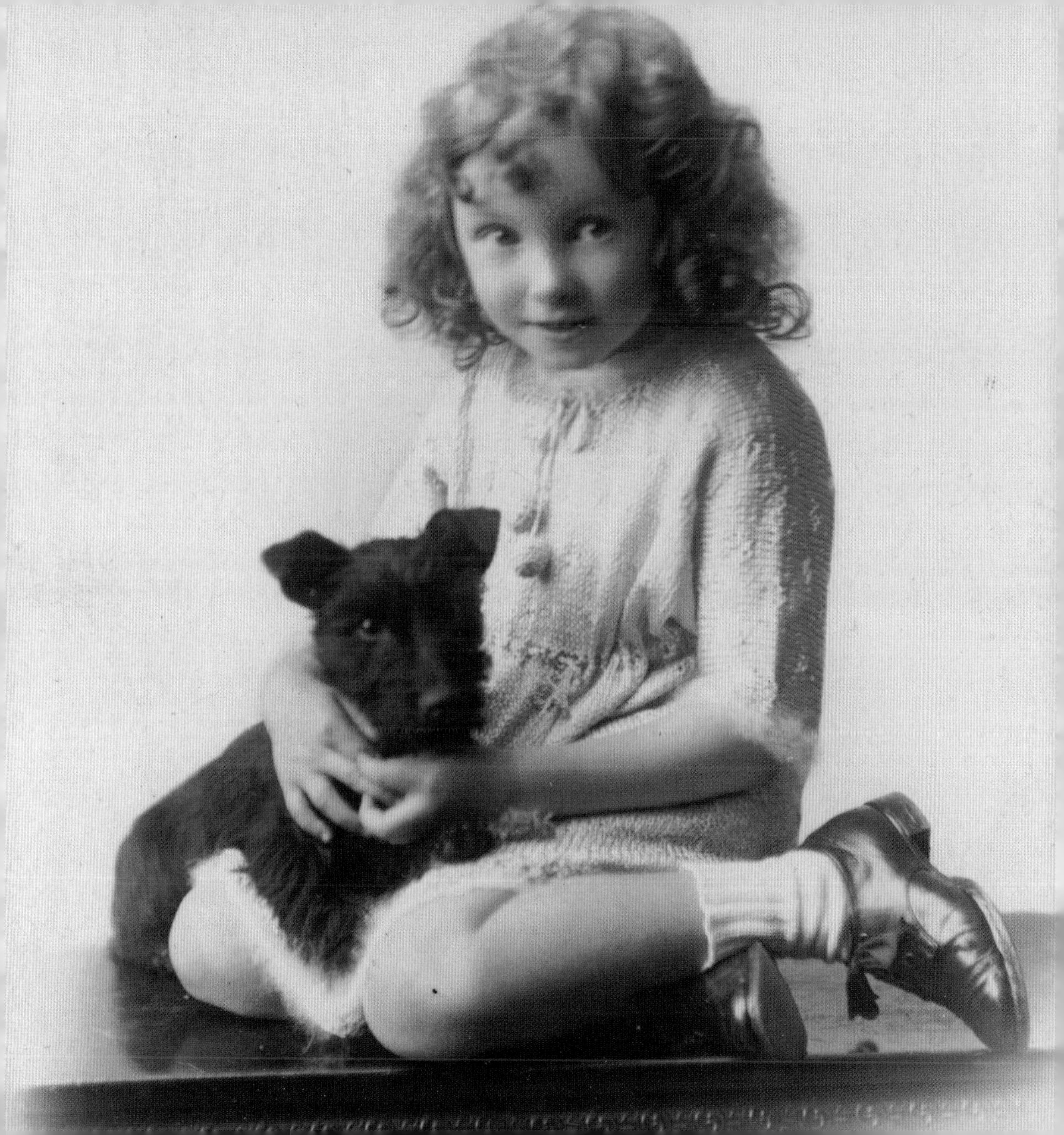

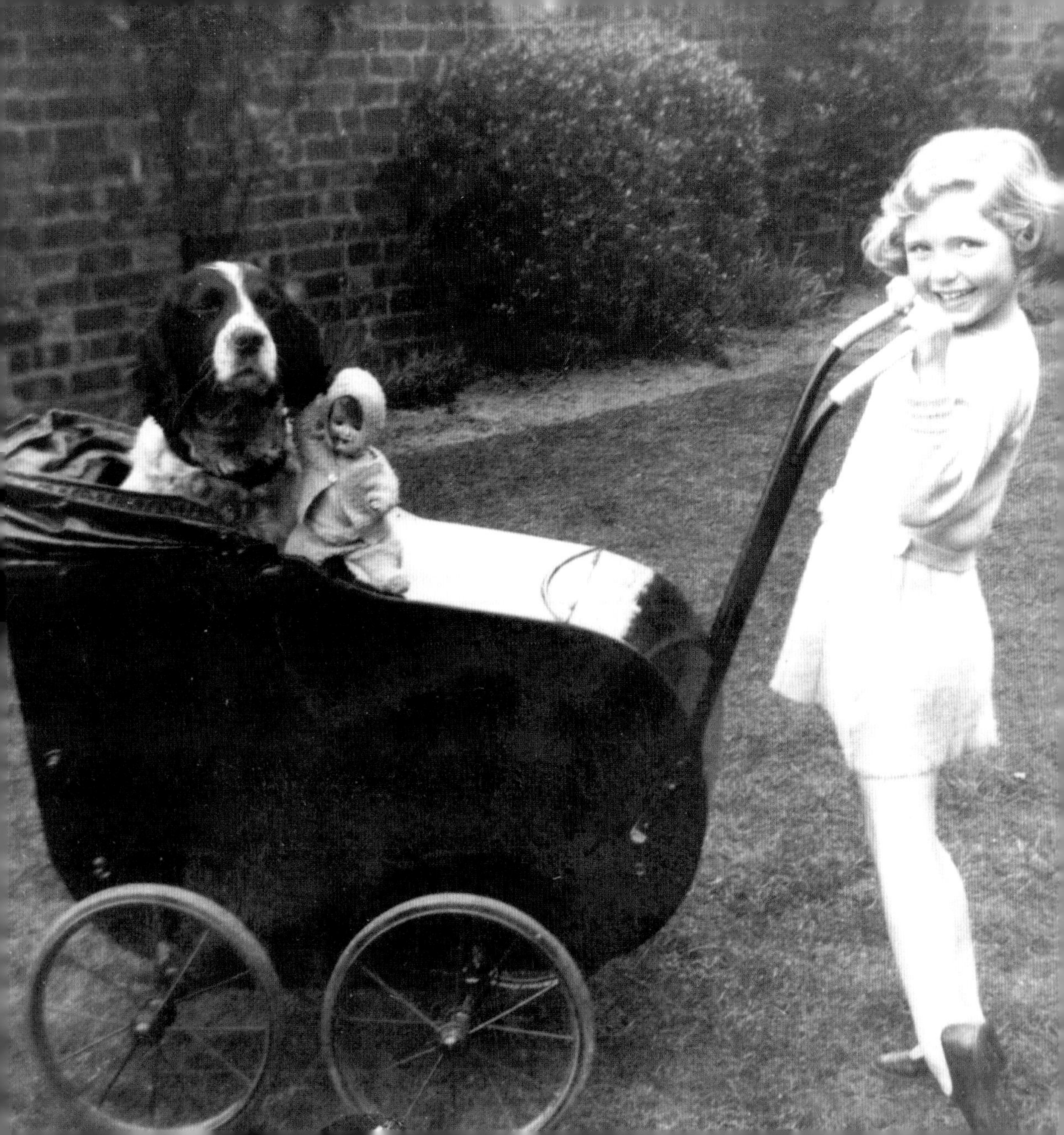

Almost all children love animals; very few are unkind to them. None would be unkind if they knew how much pleasure comes from treating the dumb creatures well. They are so grateful for little kindnesses, and have such charming ways of showing their love.

*Rough – The Story of a Dog, Herbert Strang's Readers – Grade 1, 1904*

Whoever would write the history of dogs must write the history of man, for in periods as remote as history reaches we find this animal associated with him as his useful servant.

*Dalziel's Book of Dogs*

*by Hugh Dalziel (1889)*

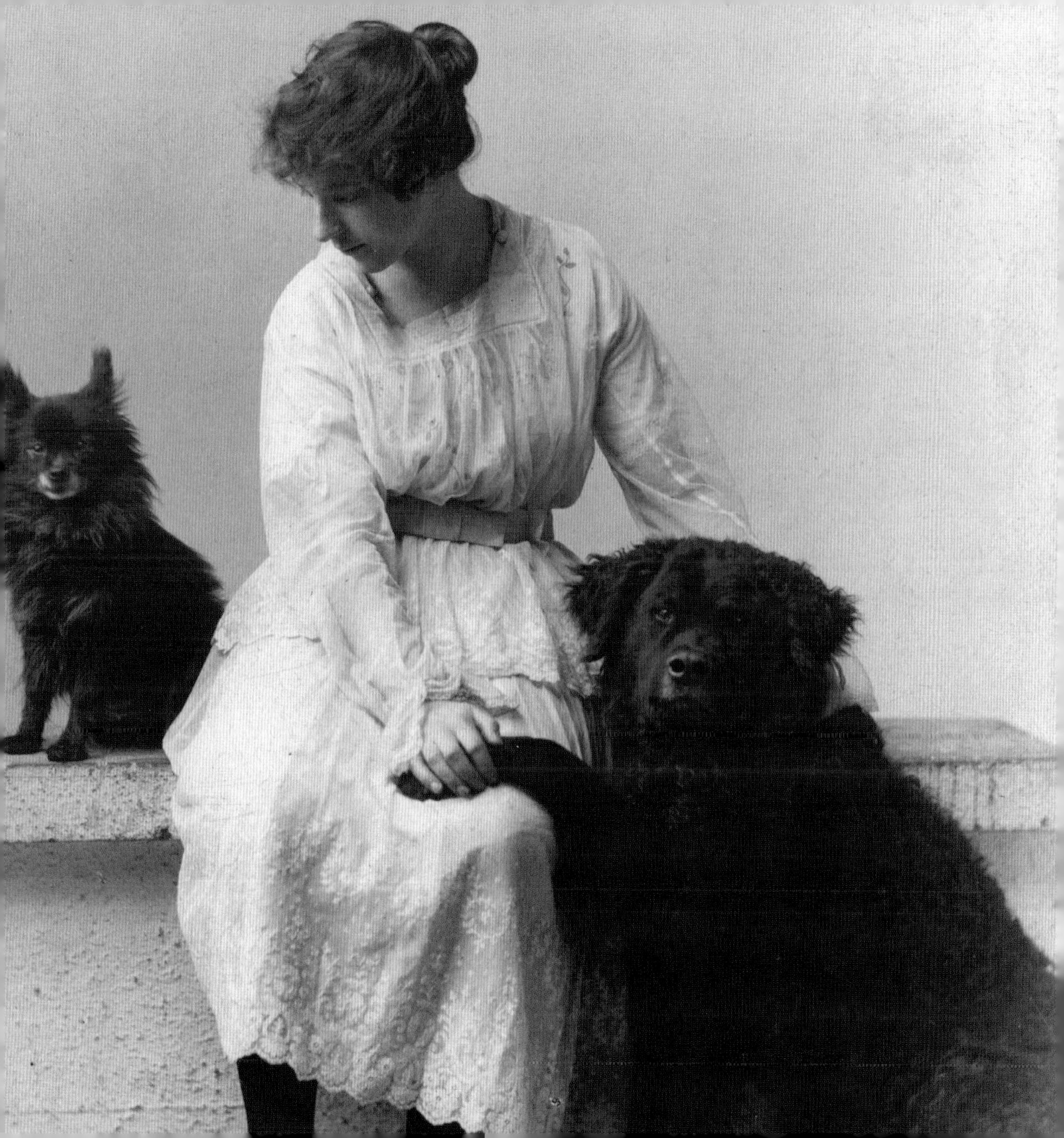

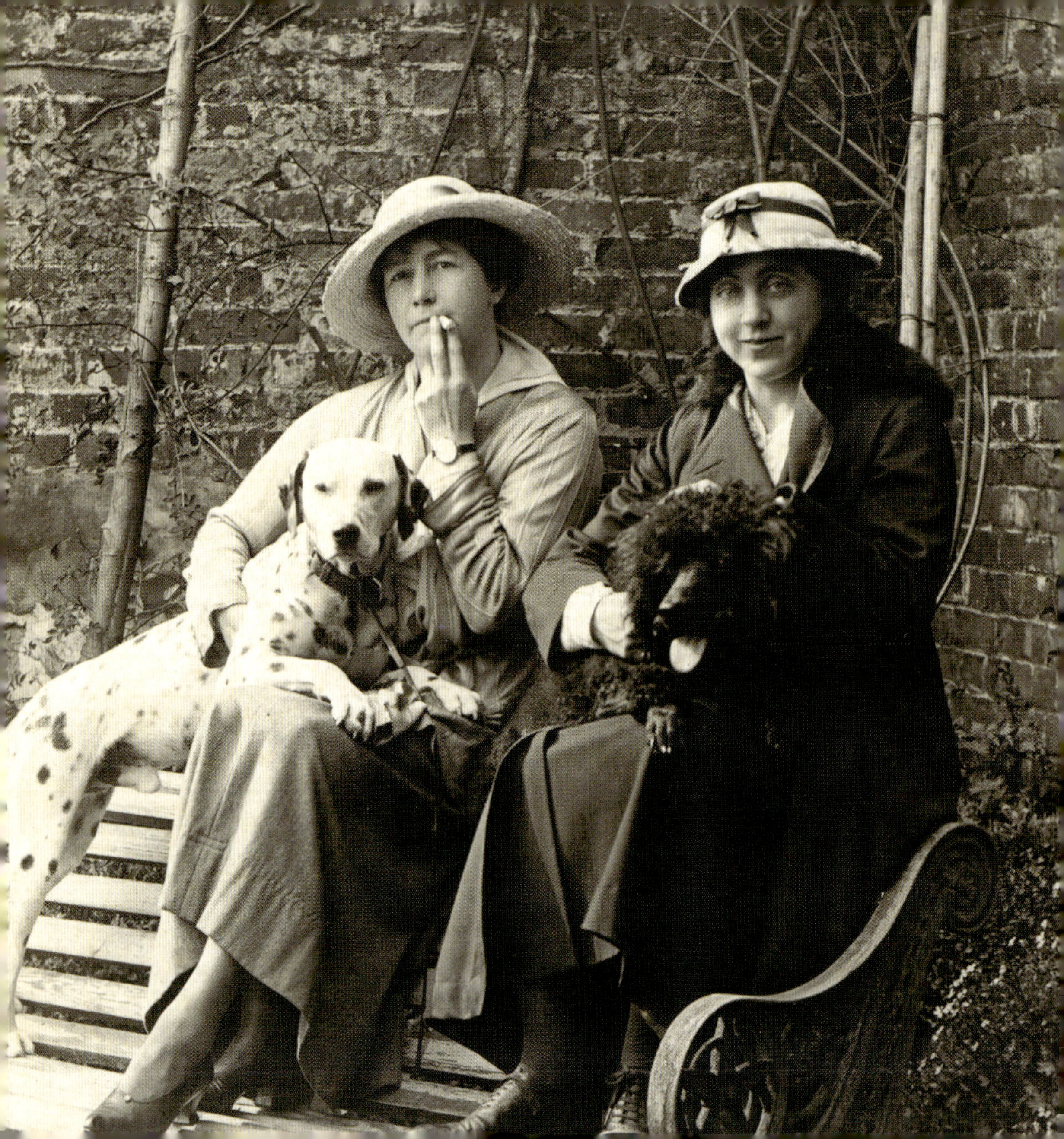

You think dogs will not be in heaven? I tell you, they will be there long before any of us.

*Robert Louis Stevenson, author*

A boy can learn a lot from a dog: obedience, loyalty, and the importance of turning around three times before lying down.

*Robert Benchley, journalist and humorist*

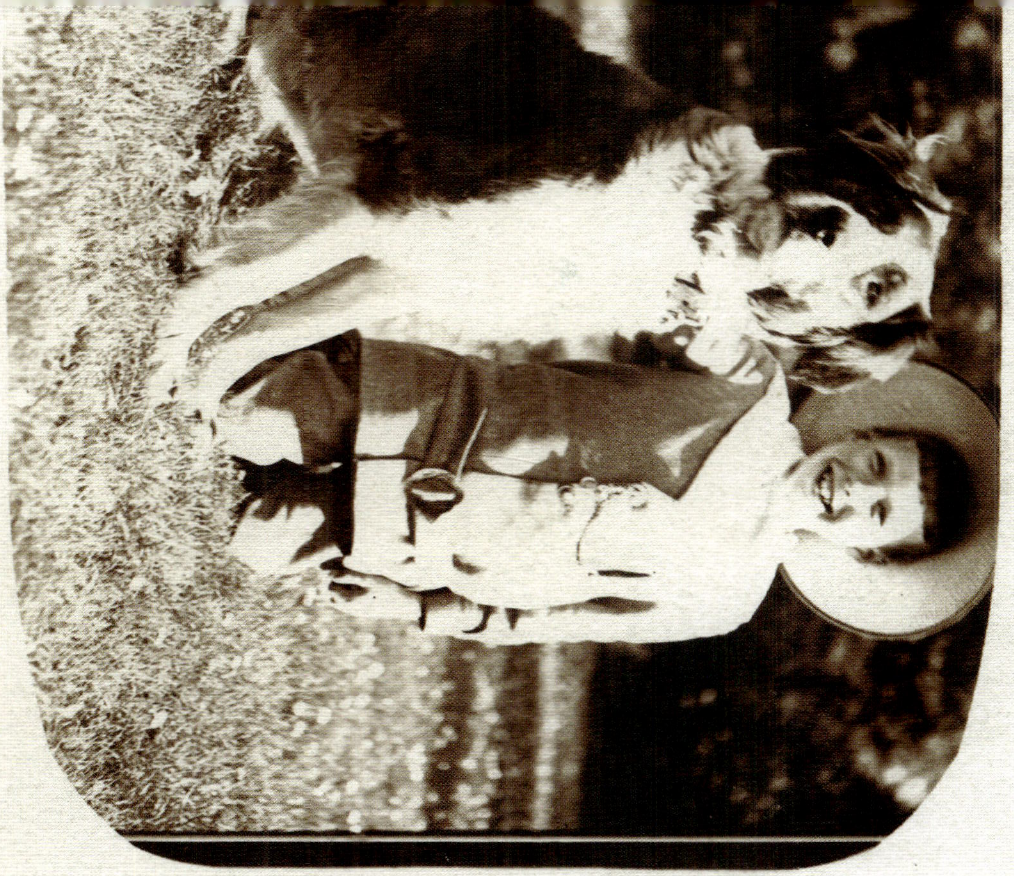

Cecil and beauty,
on the Lawn "Rocklea"
Craigendoran Scotland

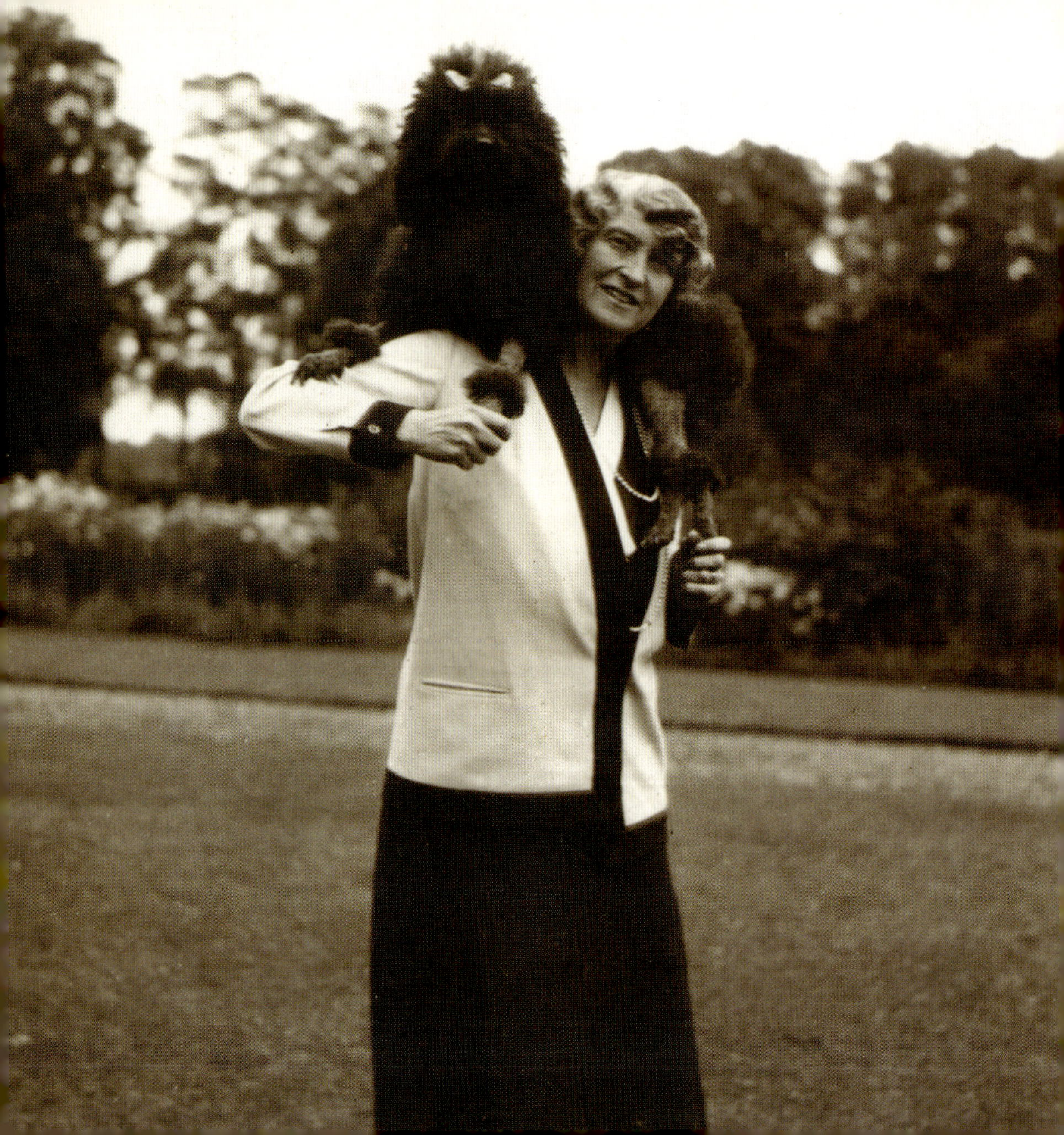

A dog reflects the family life. Whoever saw a frisky dog in a gloomy family, or a sad dog in a happy one?
Snarling people have snarling dogs, dangerous people have dangerous ones.

*Sir Arthur Conan Doyle,*

*writer and physician*

Dogs never bite me. Just humans.

*Marilyn Monroe, actress*

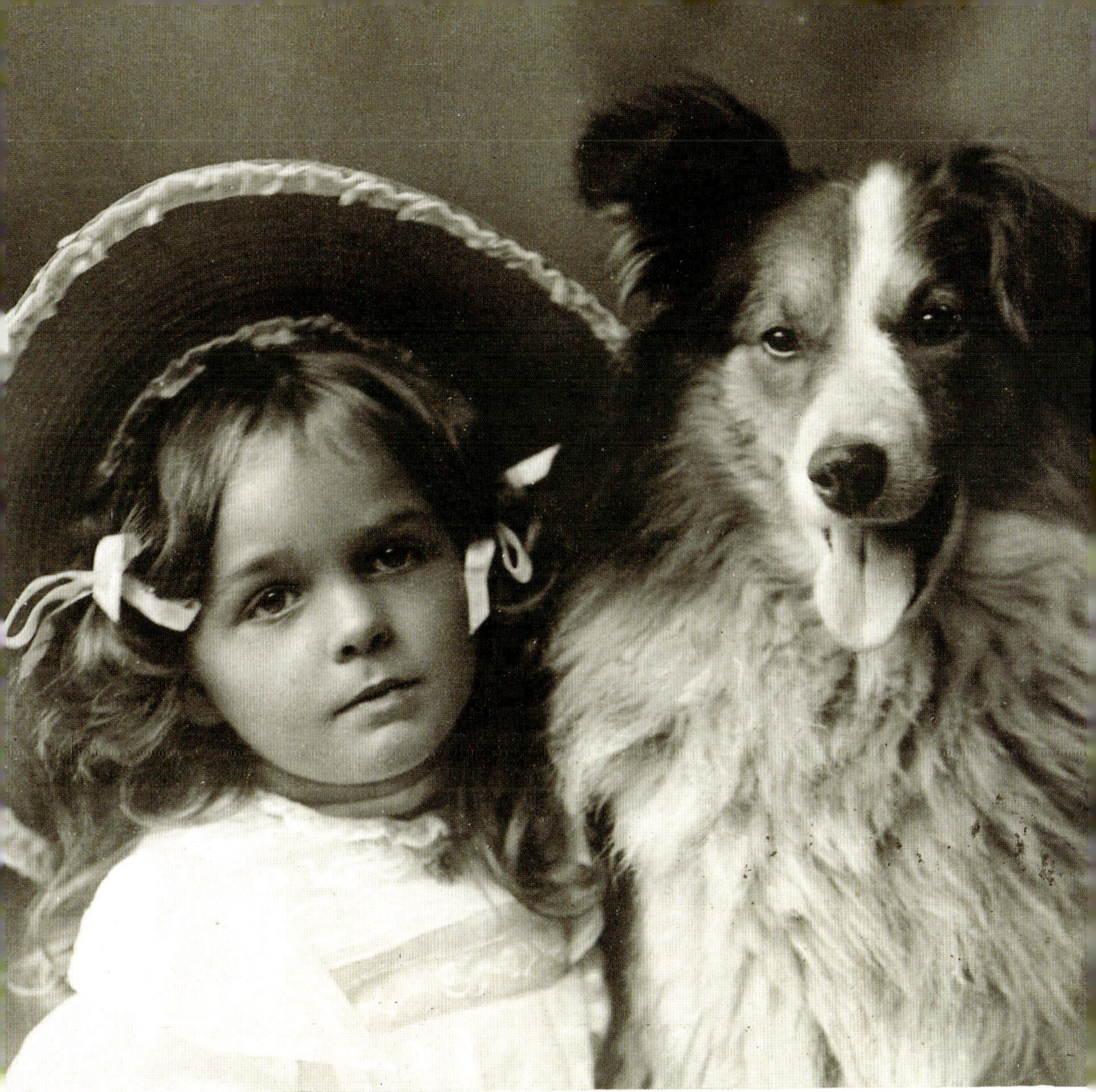

Dossie & Shep with love from Nanny

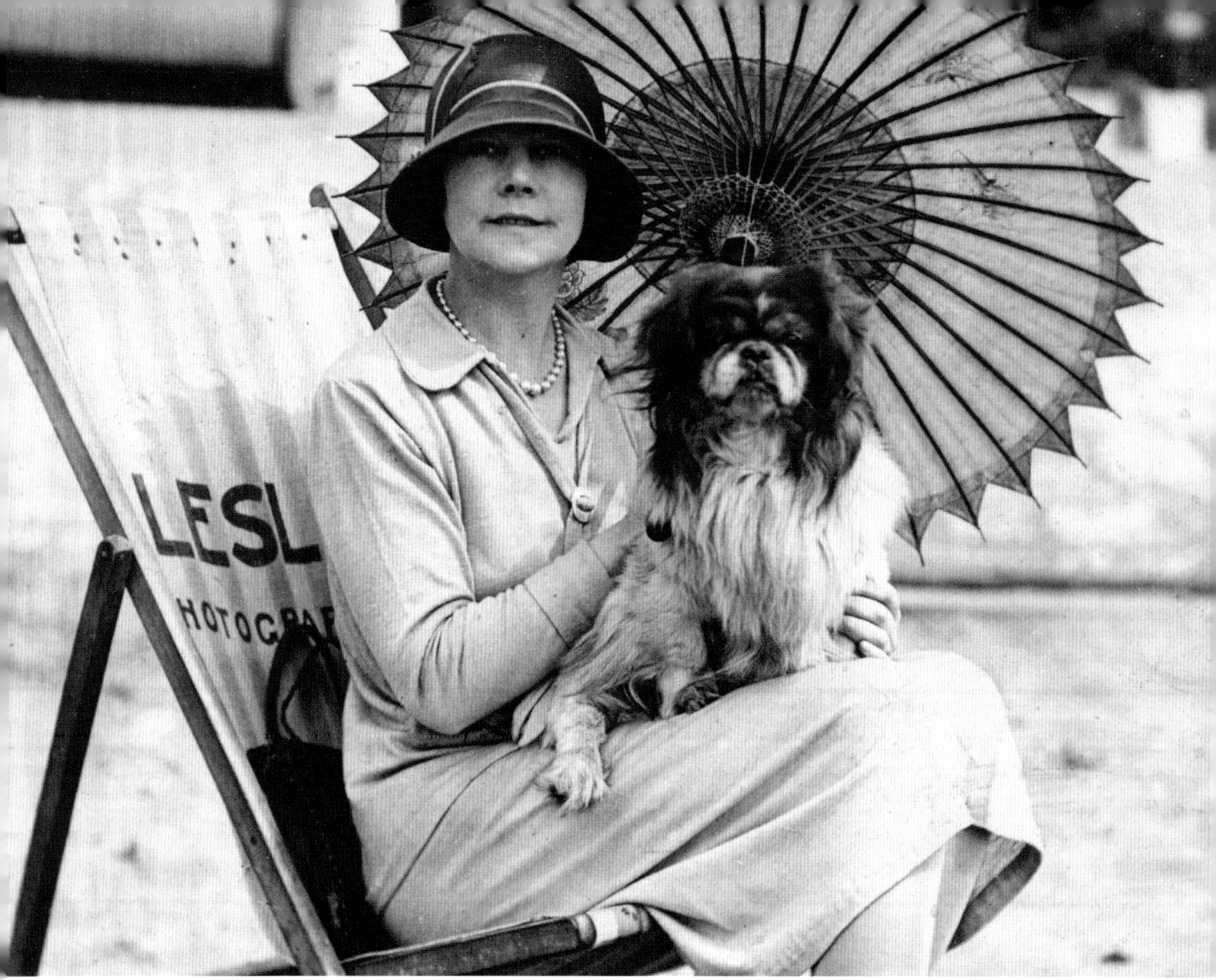


When an eighty-five pound mammal licks your tears away, then tries to sit on your lap, it's hard to feel sad.

*Kristan Higgins author, In Your Dreams*

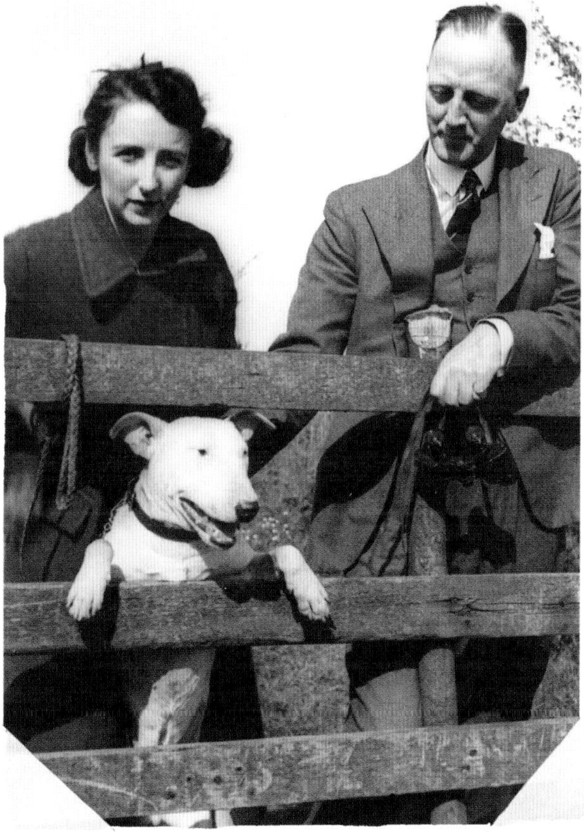

Once you have had a wonderful dog, a life without one, is a life diminished.

*Dean Koontz, author*

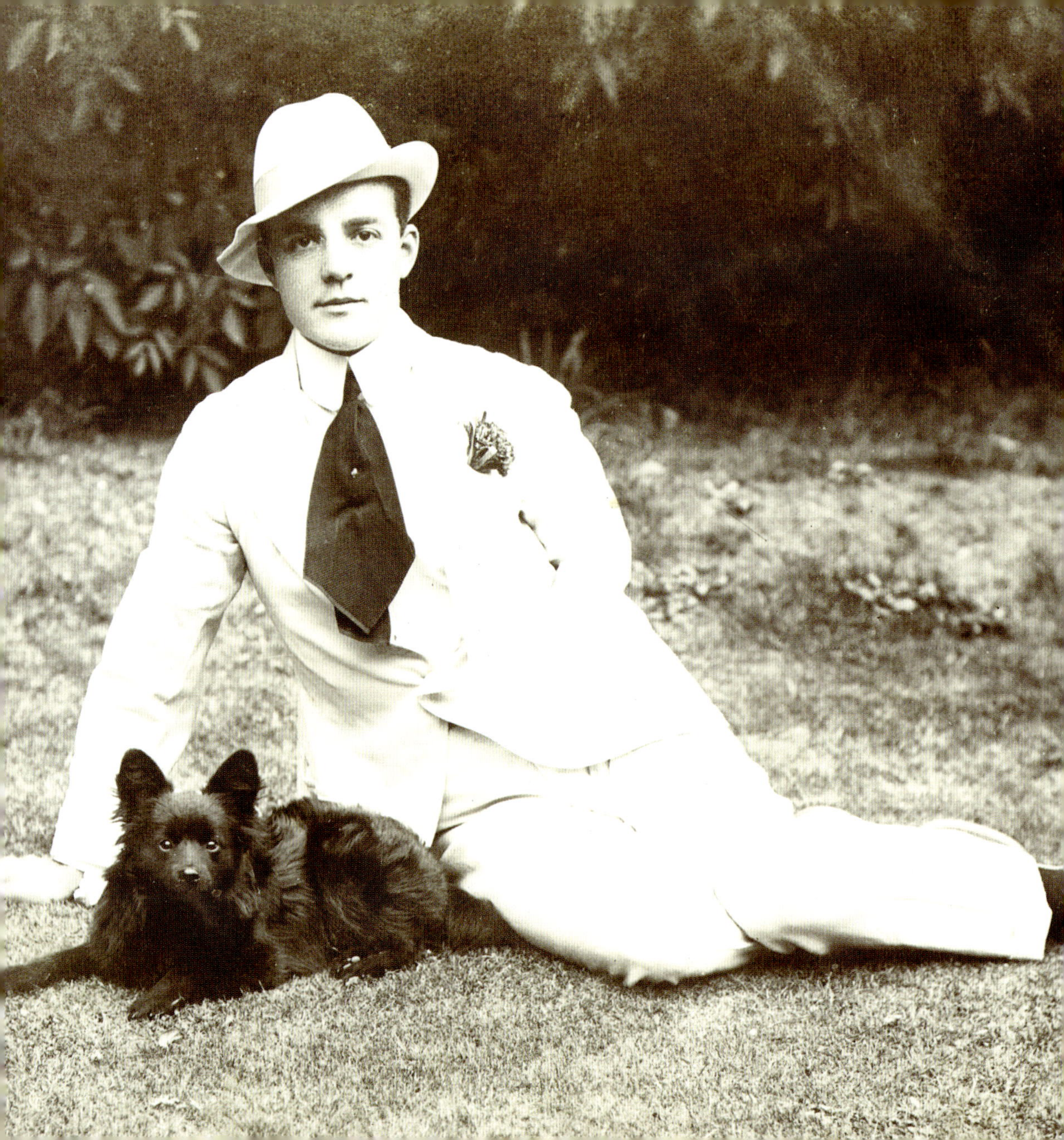

But I like Binkie my dog, because
He knows how to behave,
So, Binkie's the same as the First Friend was,
And I am the Man in the Cave.

*Rudyard Kipling, author and poet*

If you think dogs can't count, try putting three dog biscuits in your pocket and then give him only two of them.

*Phil Pastoret, author*

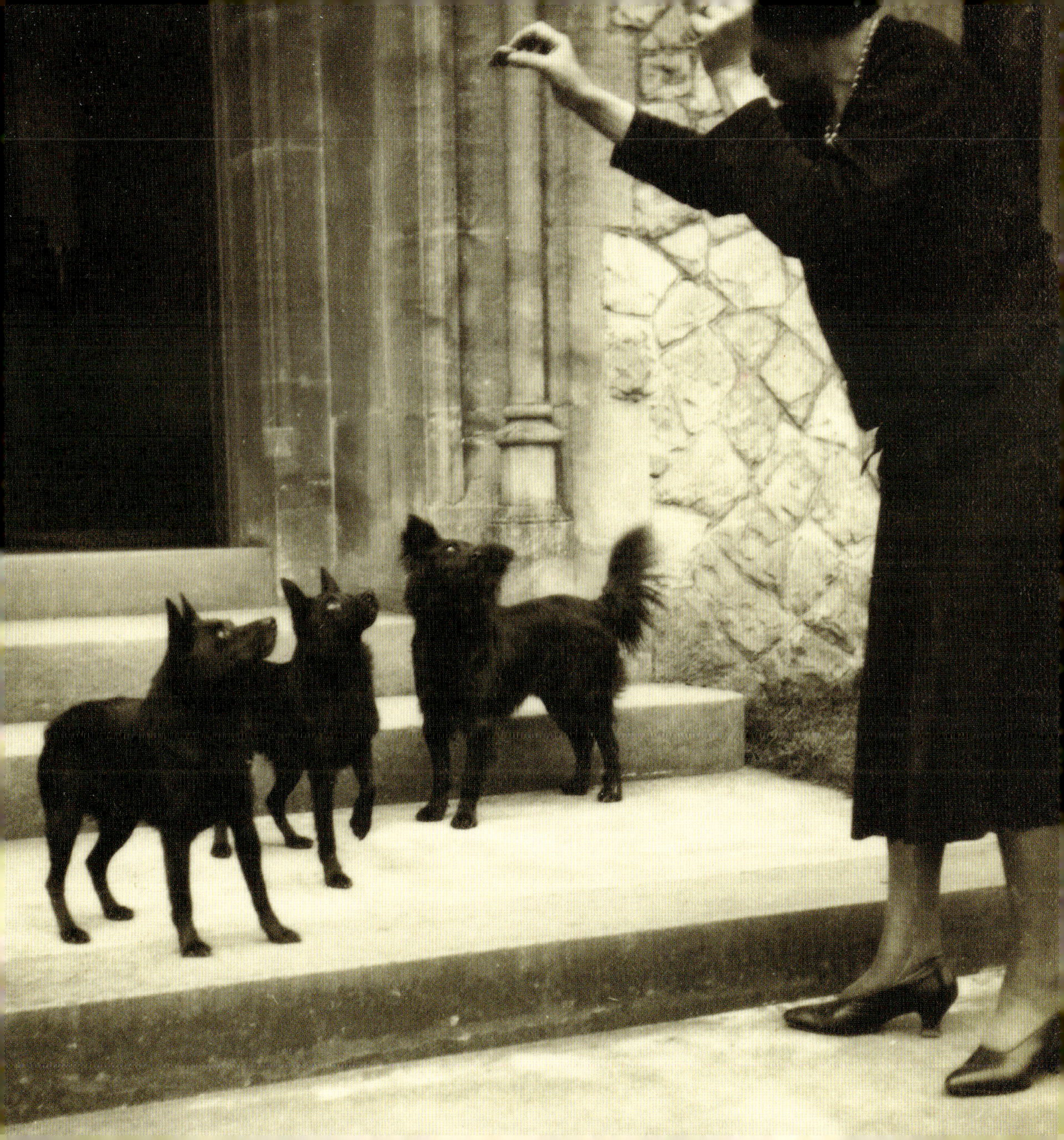

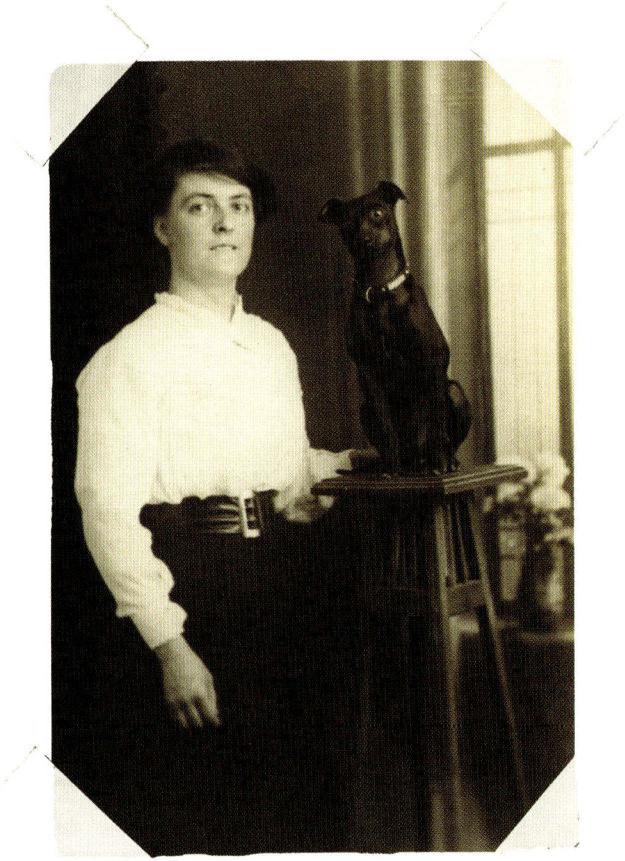

Watson: Is there any point to which you would wish to draw my attention?

Holmes: To the curious incident of the dog in the night-time.

Watson: The dog did nothing in the night-time.

Holmes: That was the curious incident.

*Sir Arthur Conan Doyle,*
*writer and physician*

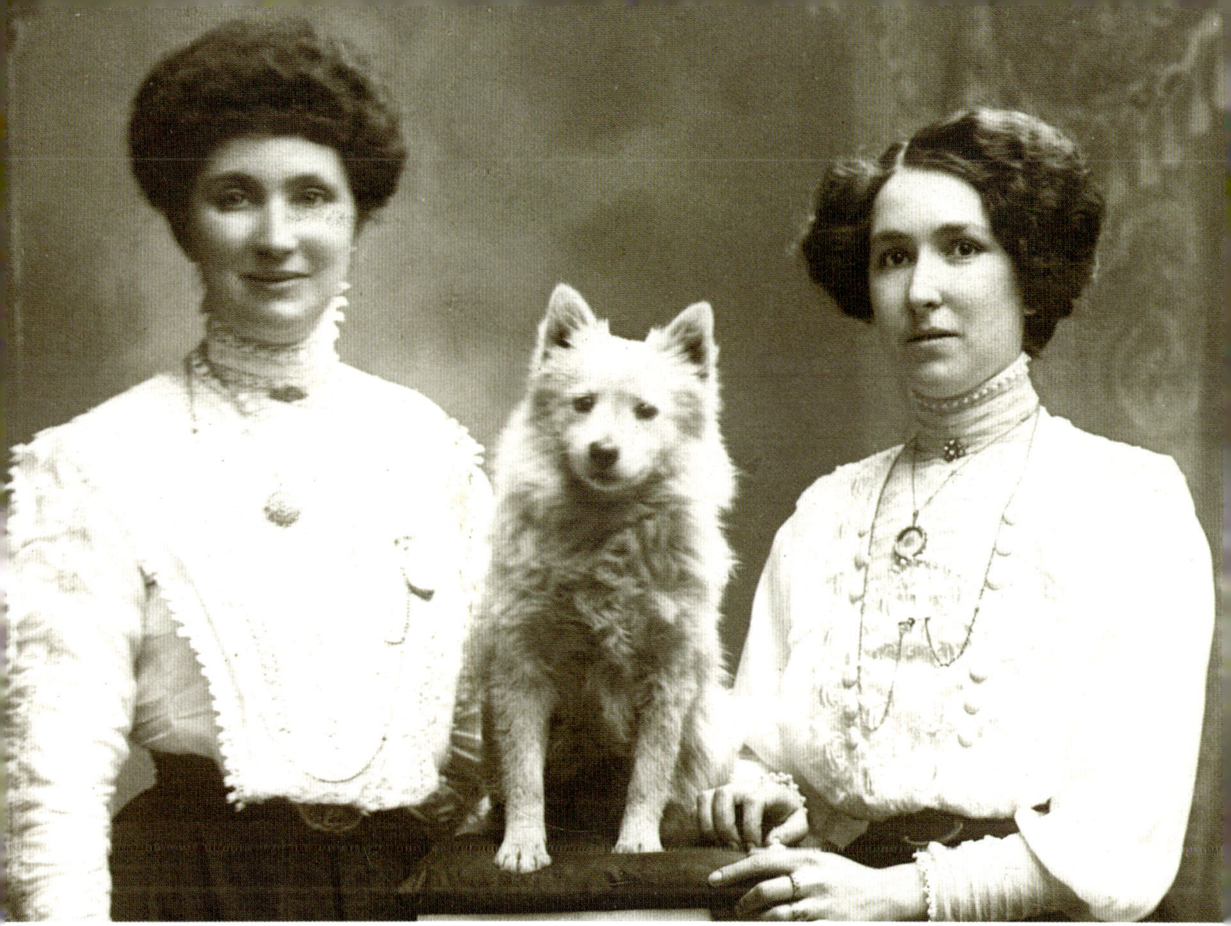

Dogs are better than human beings because they know but do not tell.

*Emily Dickinson, poet*

If you eliminate smoking and gambling, you will be amazed to find that almost all an Englishman's pleasures can be, and mostly are, shared by his dog.

*George Bernard Shaw, playwright*

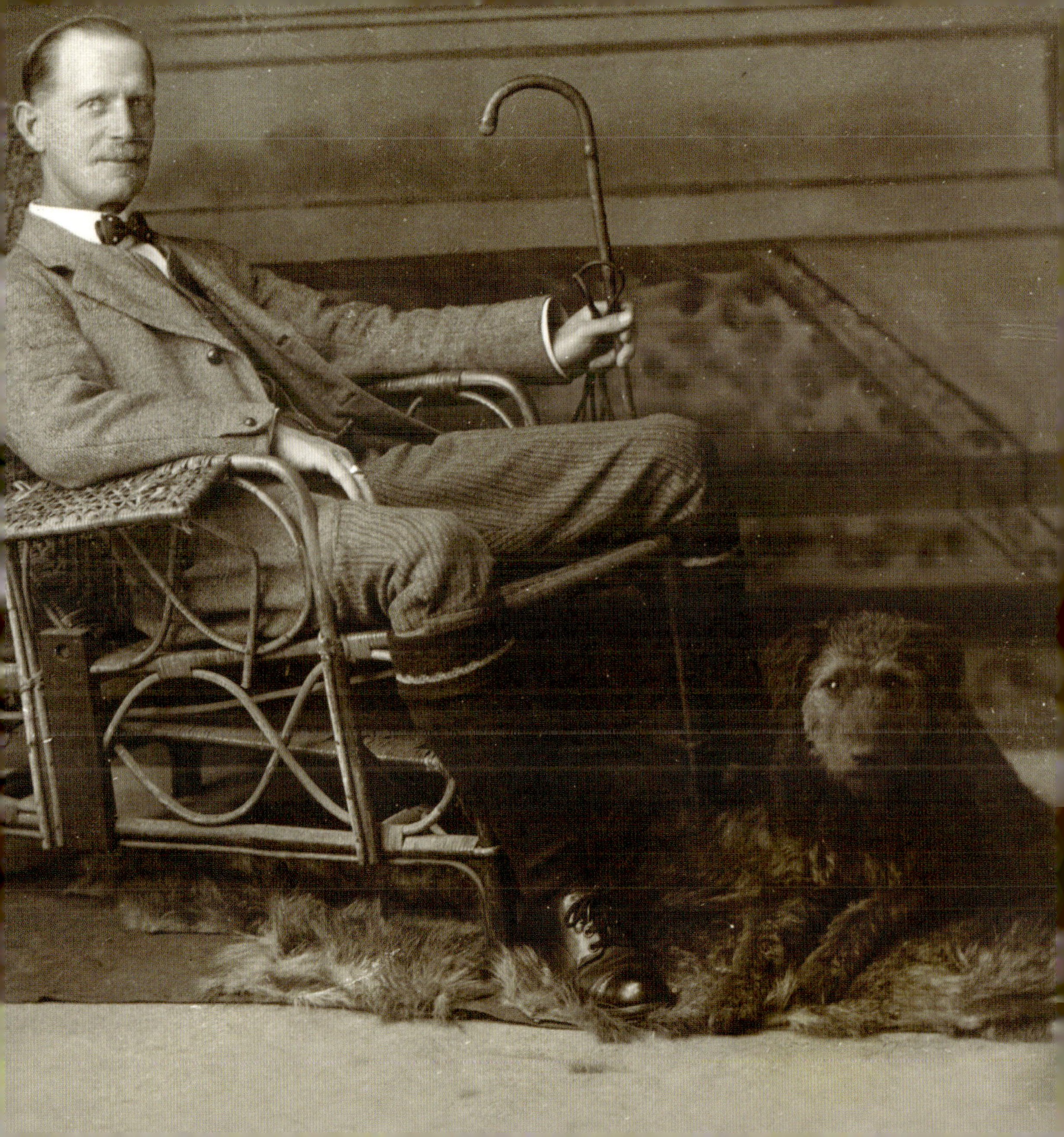

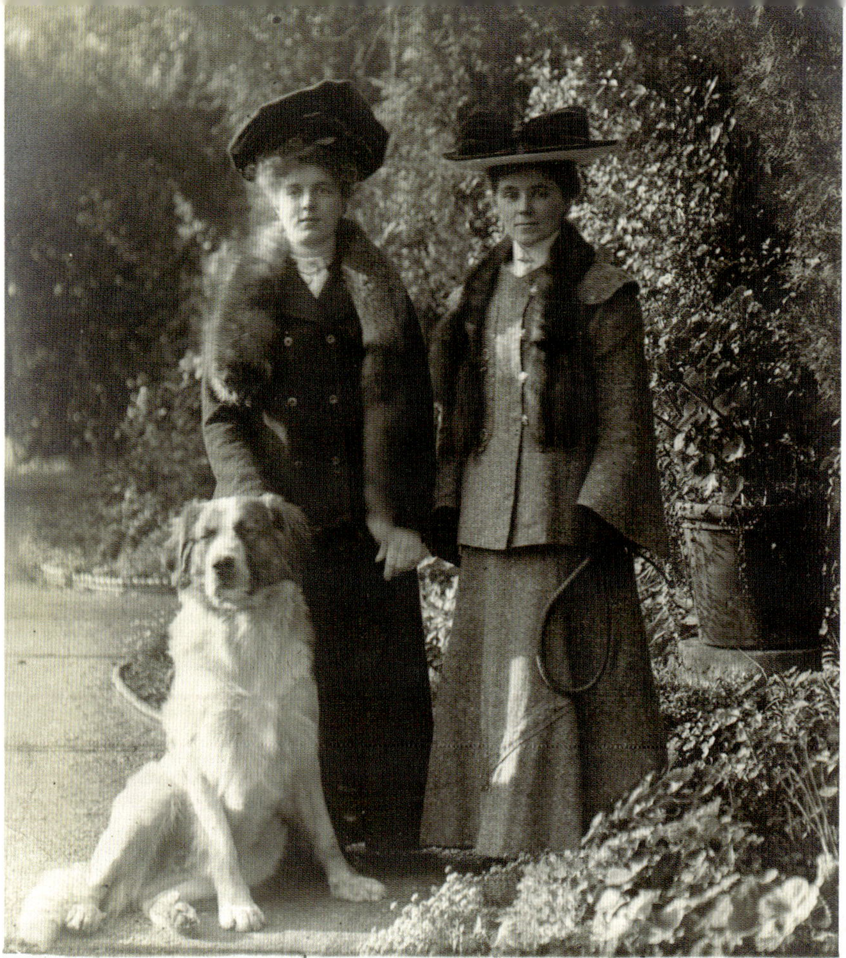

"Waverley"

With kind regards
from us three
Nov 9th 1904.

And because he loves me so,
Better than his kind will do
Often, man or woman,
Give I back more love again
Than dogs often take of men,
Leaning from my Human.

*To My Dog "Flush" by the poet  Elizabeth Barrett Browning*

There exists, however, a further species of dog, an animal whose ability to inspire love and render faithful service is equal to that of any of the 92 breeds already mentioned, but whose name will not be found within the august pages of the Kennel Club Stud Book. I refer to that lovable but indeterminate animal, the mongrel.

*'Everyman's Dog' by Major Mitford Brice,*
*publ. Cooper, McDougall & Robertson*

---

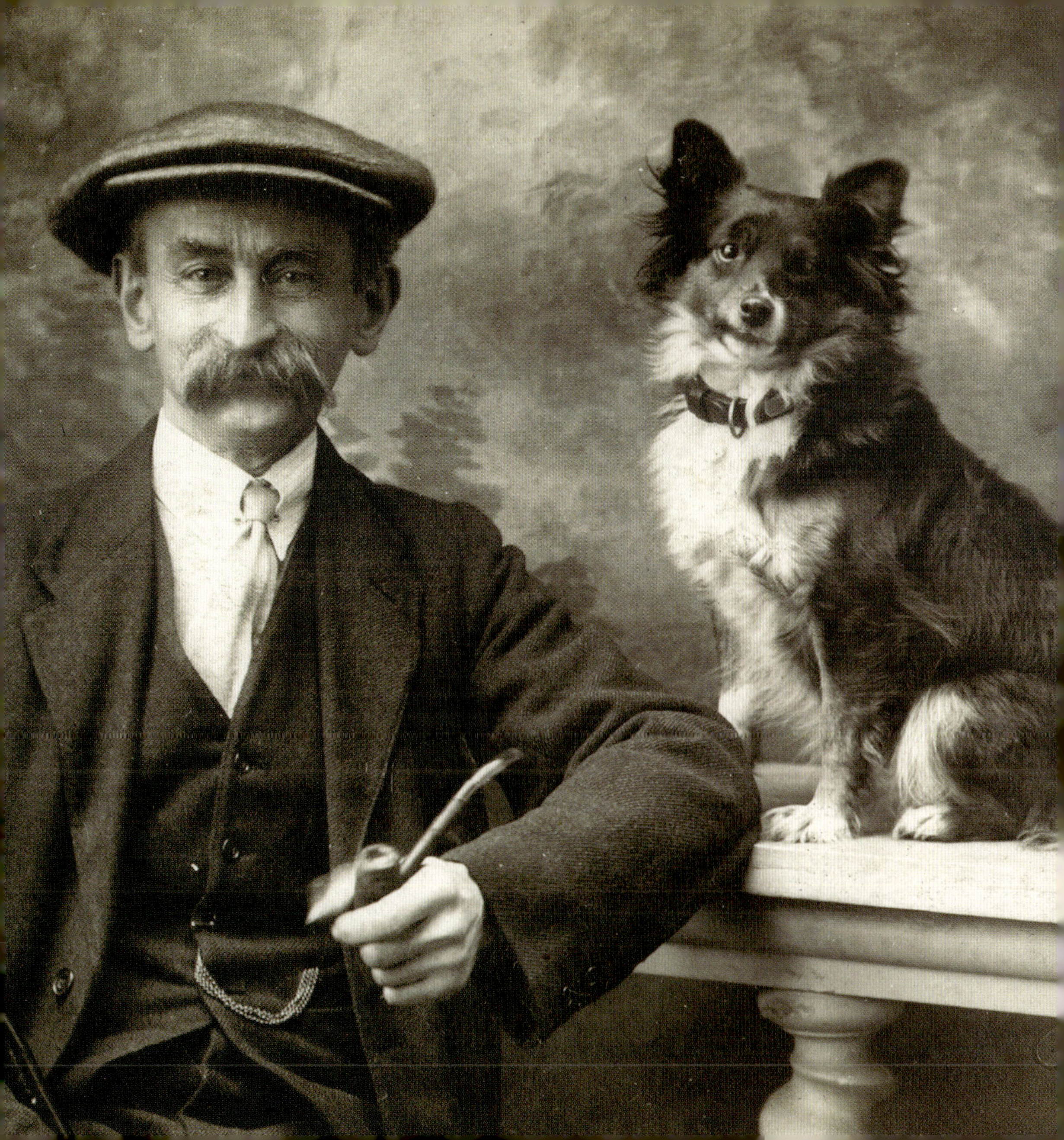

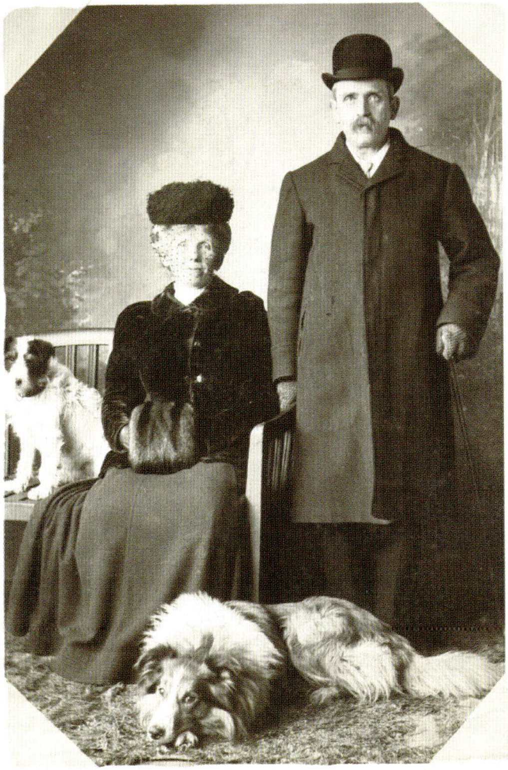

Let sleeping dogs lie.

*Robert Walpole, first Prime Minister of Great Britain*

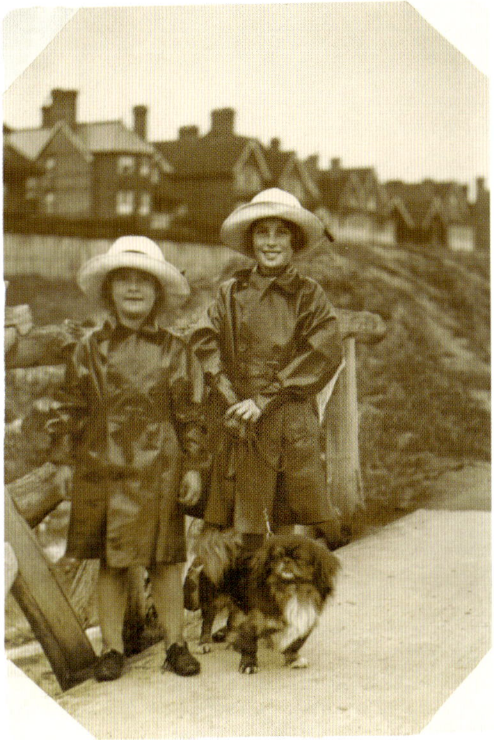

O mistress mine,
where are you roaming?

*William Shakespeare, Twelfth Night*

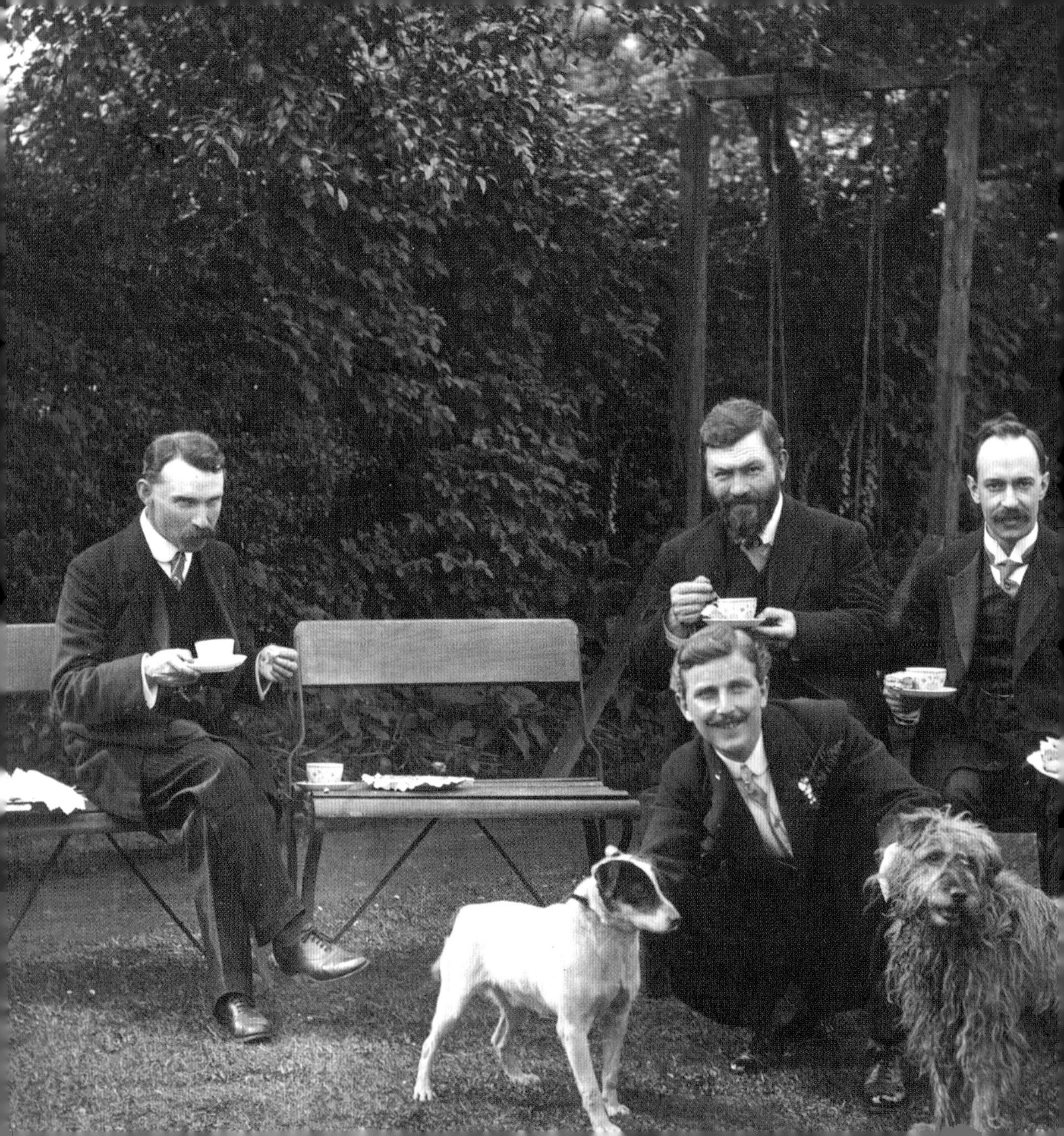

To his dog, every man is Napoleon; hence the constant popularity of dogs.

*Aldous Huxley, author and philosopher*

The world would be a nicer place if everyone had the ability to love as unconditionally as a dog.

*M.K. Clinton, author*

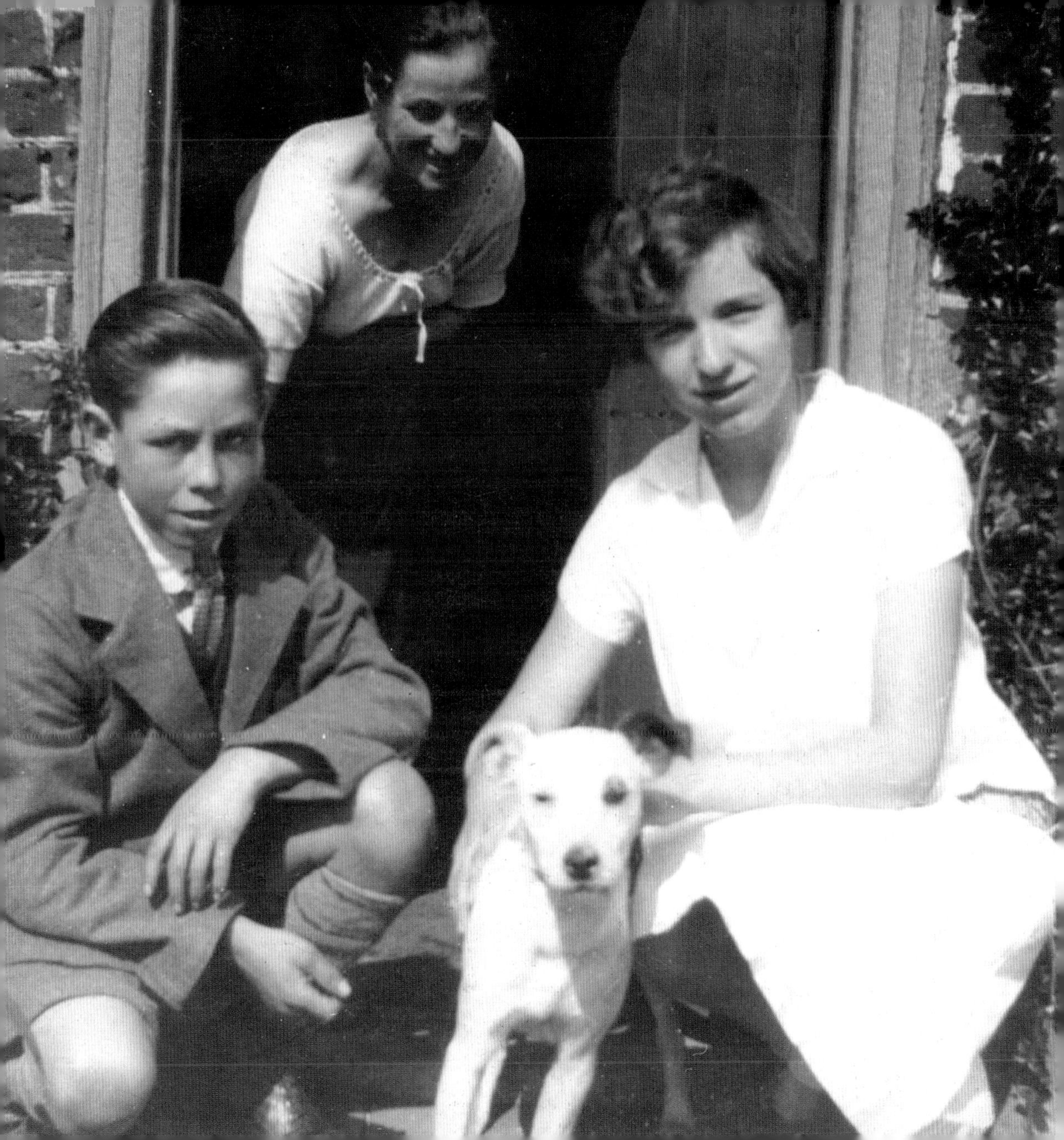

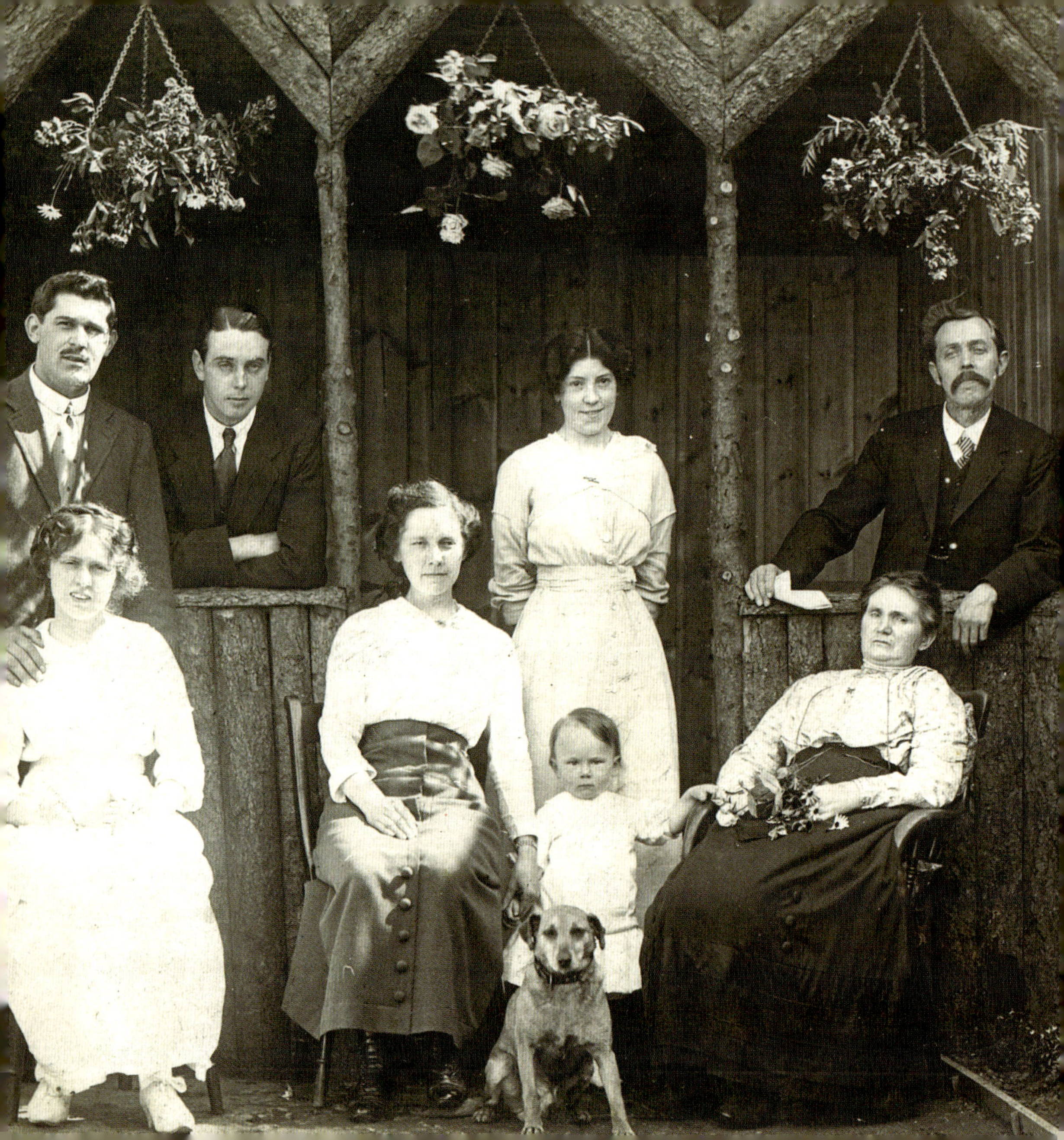

He wa'n't no common dog, he wa'n't no mongrel; he was a composite. A composite dog is a dog that is made up of all the valuable qualities that's in the dog breed—kind of a syndicate; and a mongrel is made up of all riffraff that's left over.

*Mark Twain, author and humorist*

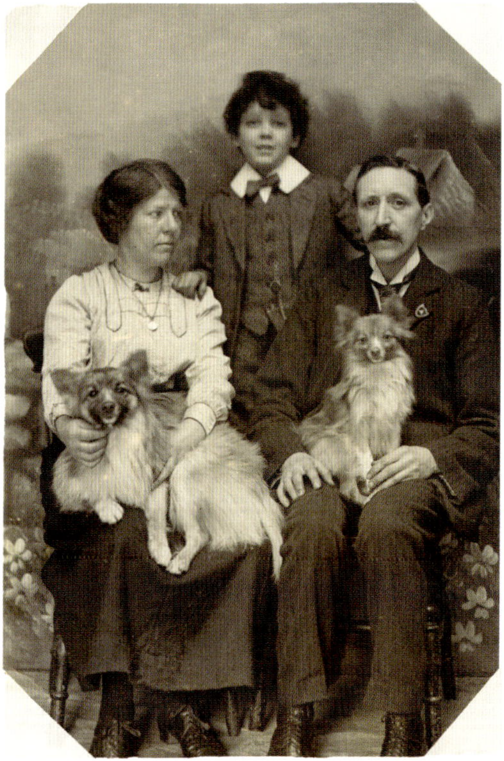

If a dog will not come to you after having looked you in the face, you should go home and examine your conscience.

*Woodrow Wilson, 28th President of the United States*

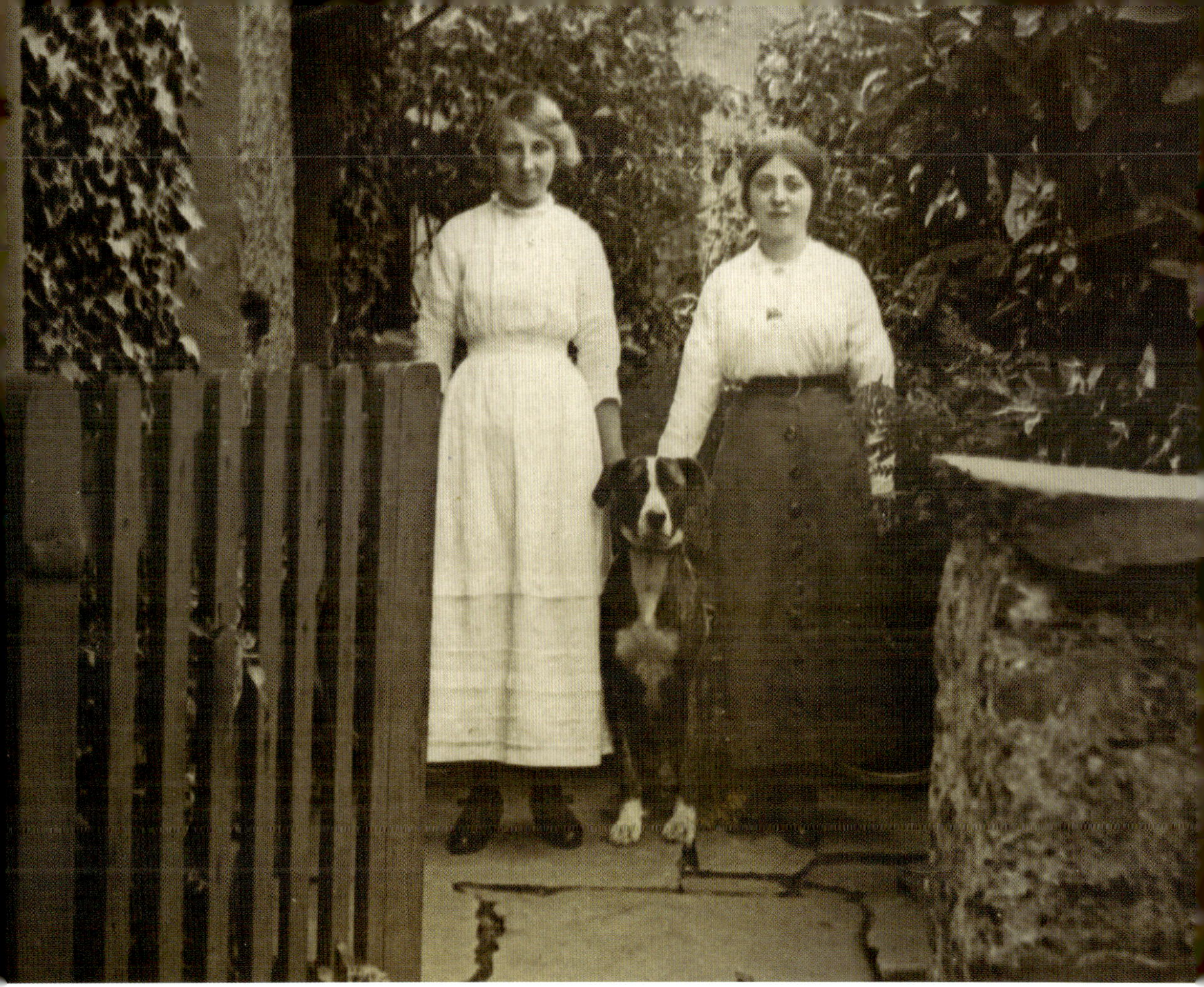

Outside of a dog, a book is man's best friend. Inside of a dog it's too dark to read.

*Groucho Marx,*
*actor and humorist*

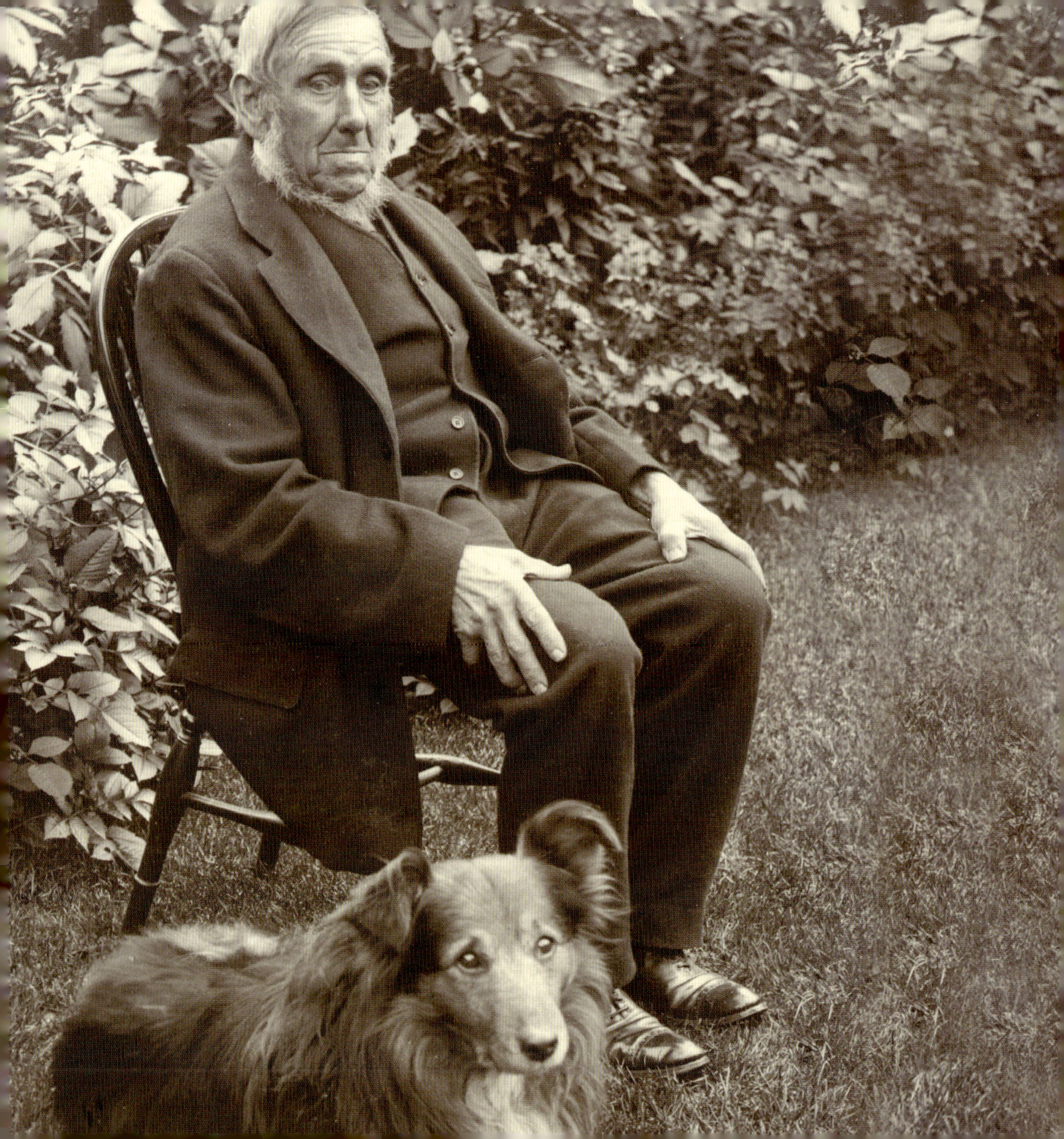

Near this spot are deposited the remains of one who possessed Beauty without Vanity, Strength without Insolence, Courage without Ferocity, and all the Virtues of Man without his Vices. This praise, which would be unmeaning Flattery, if inscribed over human ashes, is but a just Tribute to the Memory of BOATSWAIN, a Dog.

*John Cam Hobhouse,*

*politician and diarist*

Dogs don't rationalize. They don't hold anything against a person. They don't see the outside of a human but the inside of a human.

*Cesar Millan, dog 'whisperer'*

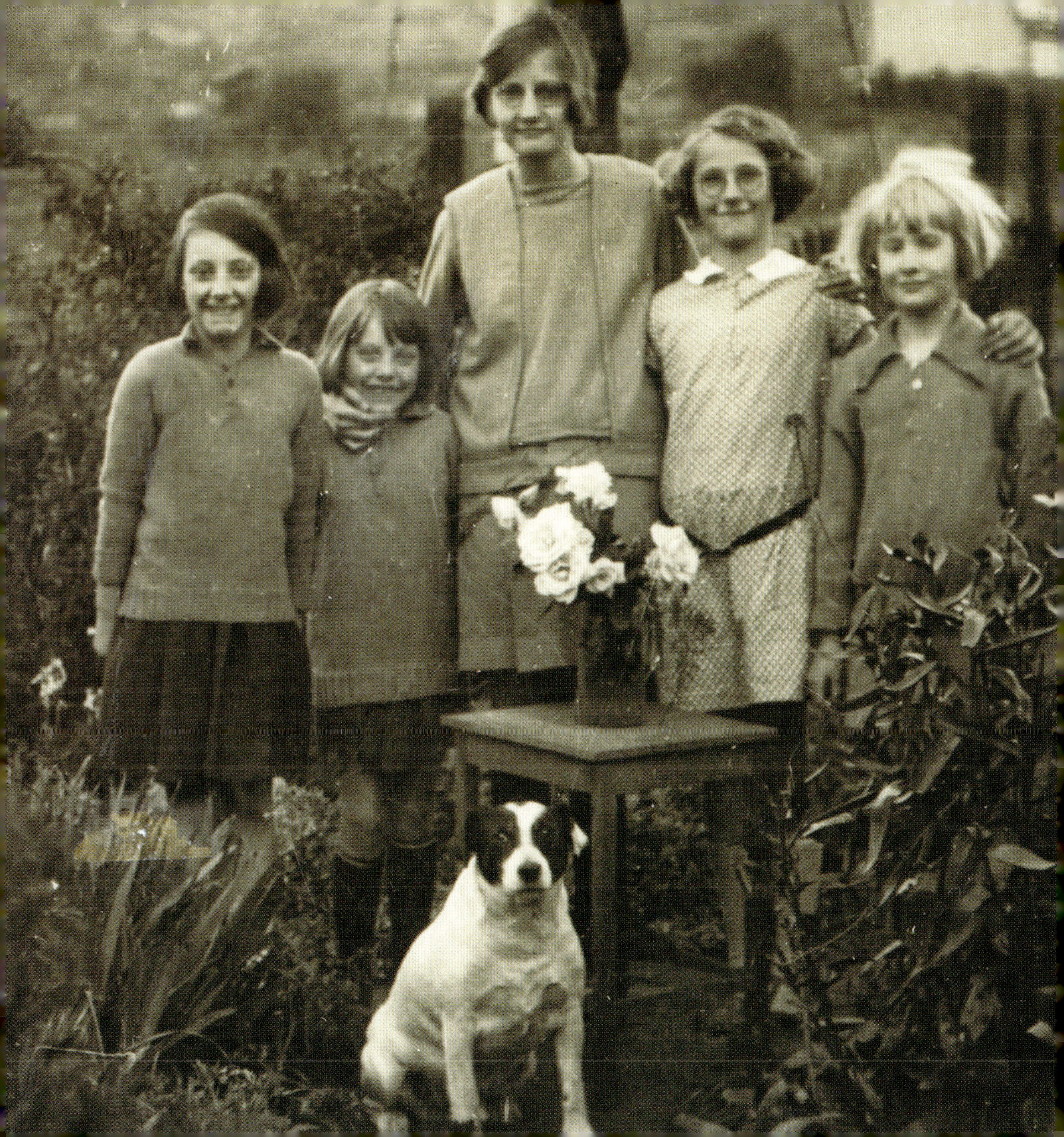

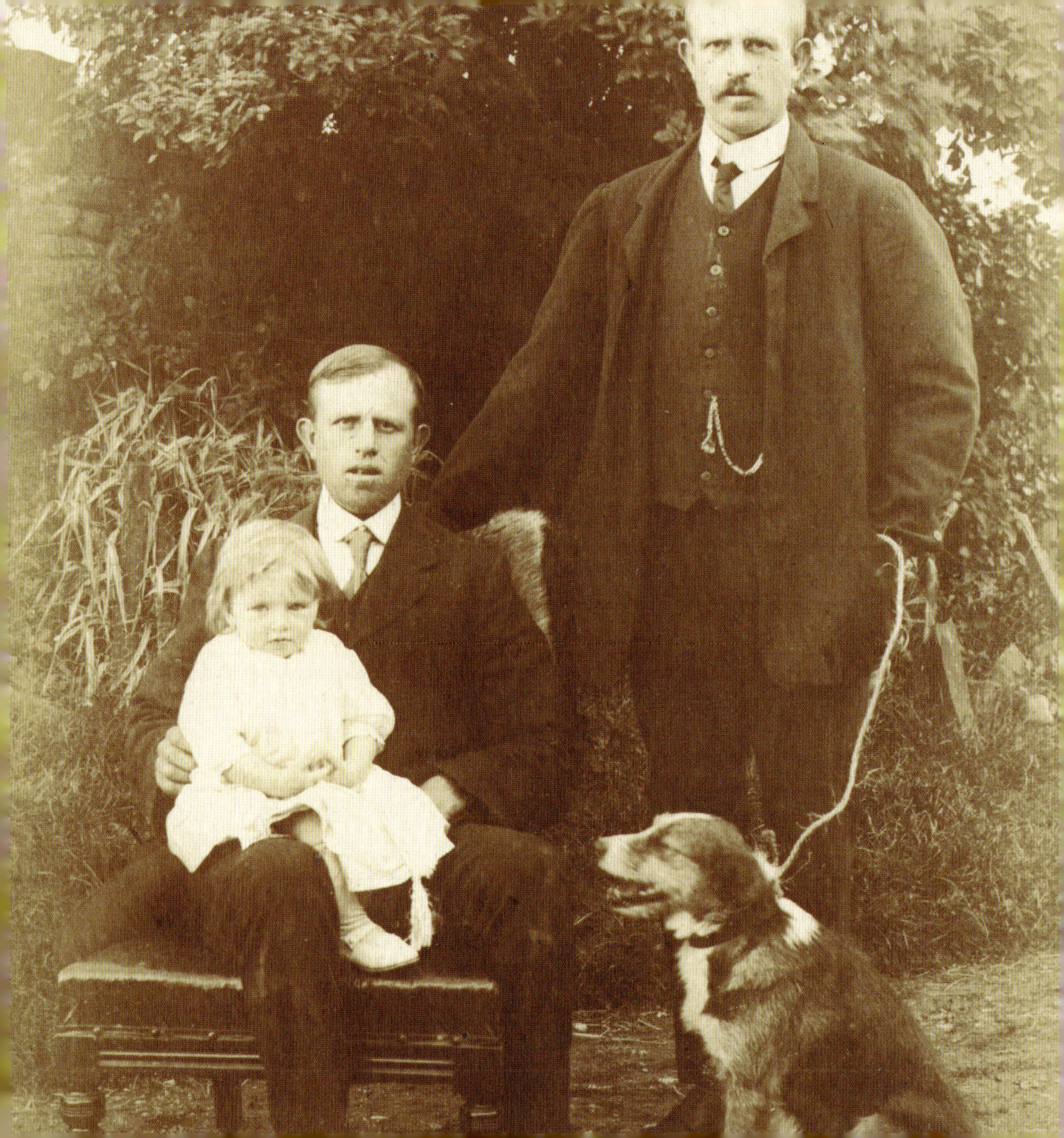

The character, sensibilities, and intellectual faculties of animals have always been a favourite study, and they are, perhaps, more strongly developed in the dog than in any other quadruped, from the circumstance of his being the constant companion of man... the more the character of the dog is known, the better his treatment is likely to be, and the stronger the sympathy excited in his behalf.

*Anecdotes of Dogs by Edward Jesse, 1846*

I think Crab, my dog, be the sourest-natured dog that lives: my mother weeping, my father wailing, my sister crying, our maid howling, our cat wringing her hands, and all our house in a great perplexity, yet did not this cruel-hearted cur shed one tear: he is a stone, a very pebble stone, and has no more pity in him than a dog:
Two Gentlemen of Verona, II.iii

*William Shakespeare, The Two Gentlemen of Verona*

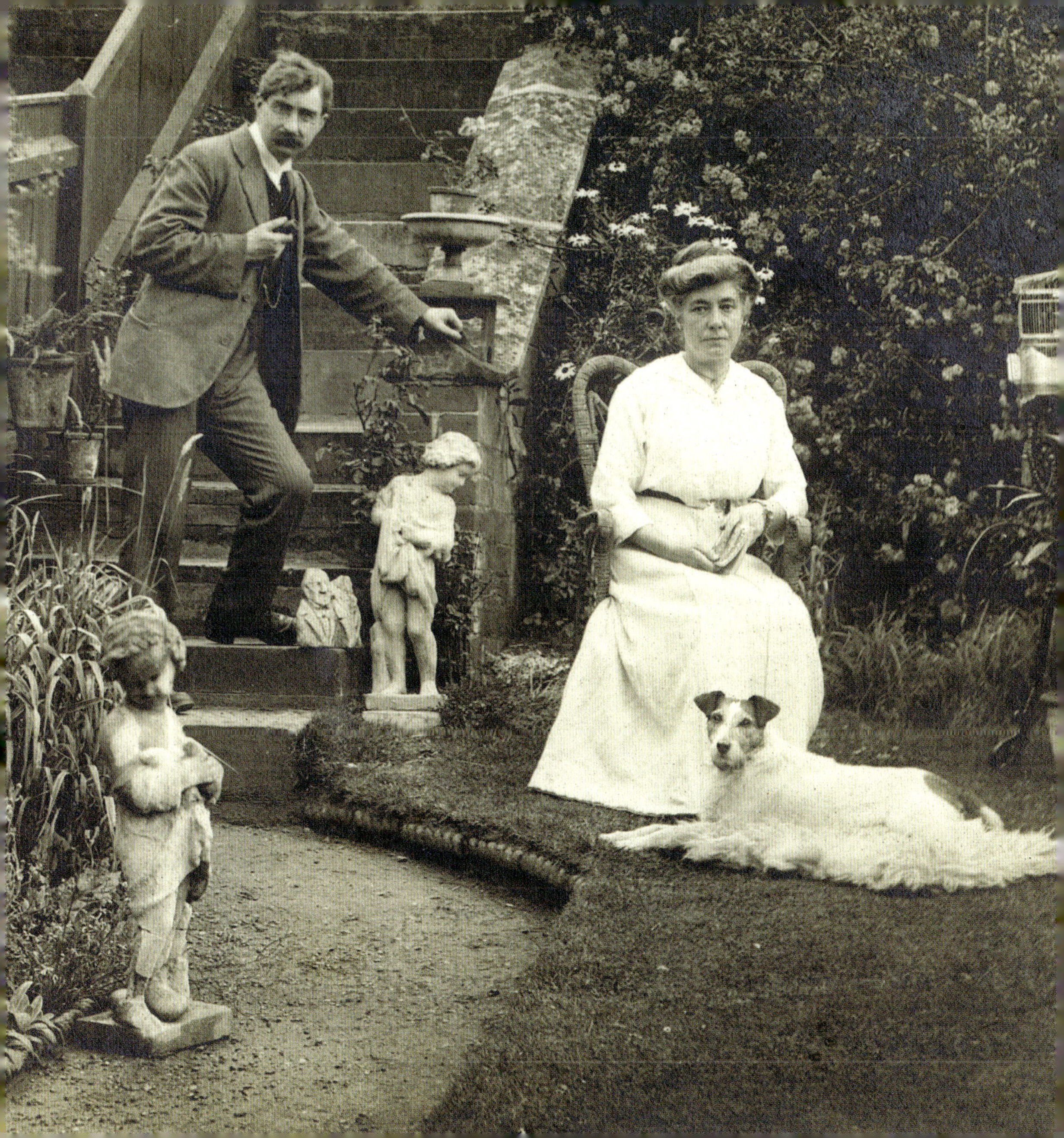

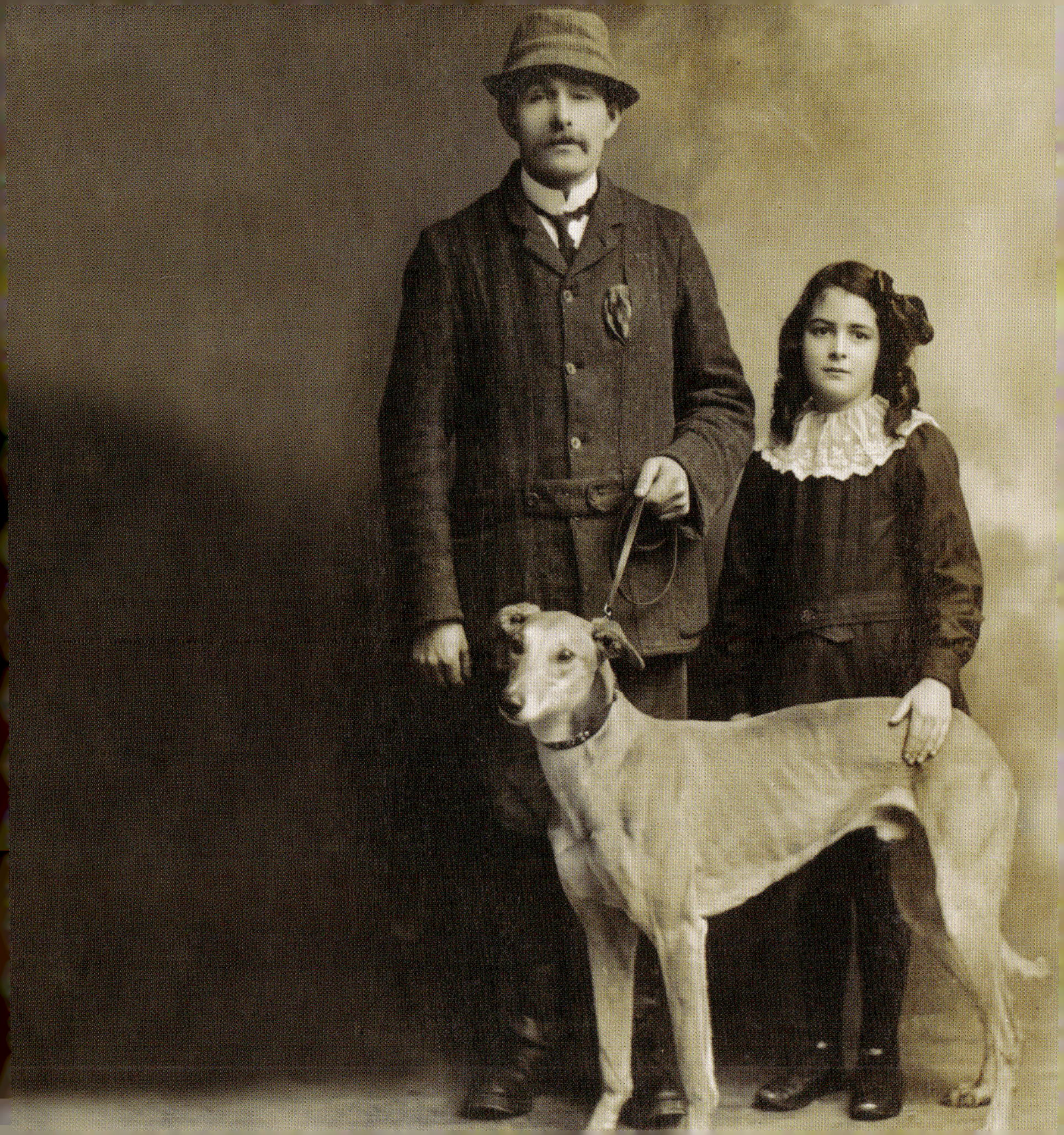

Not long after Tray did the
Shepherd remain,
Who oft o'er his grave with true
sorrow would bend;
And when dying, thus feebly was
heard the poor swain,
'O bury me, Neighbours, beside my
old friend.'

*The Old Shepherd's Dog by John Walcot*

*aka 'Peter Pinder'*

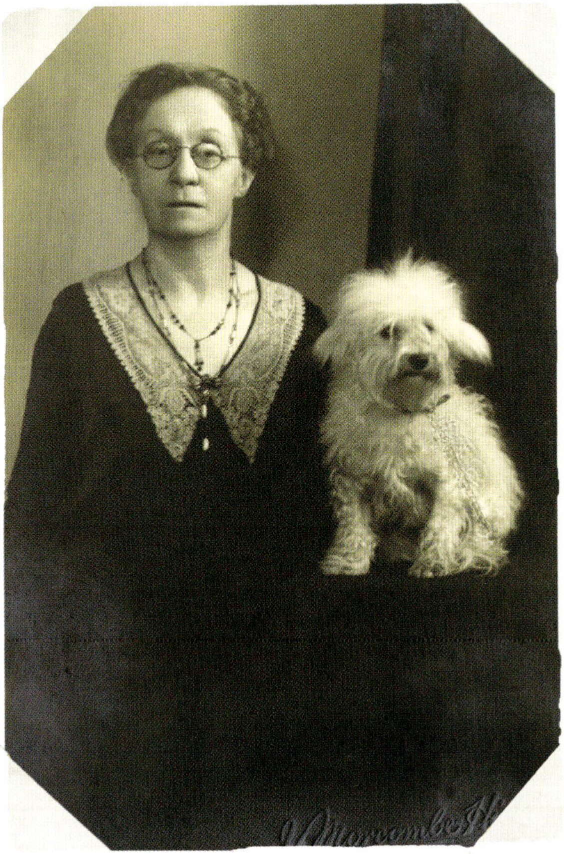

If there are no dogs in Heaven, then when I die I want to go where they went.

*Will Rogers, actor, humourist*

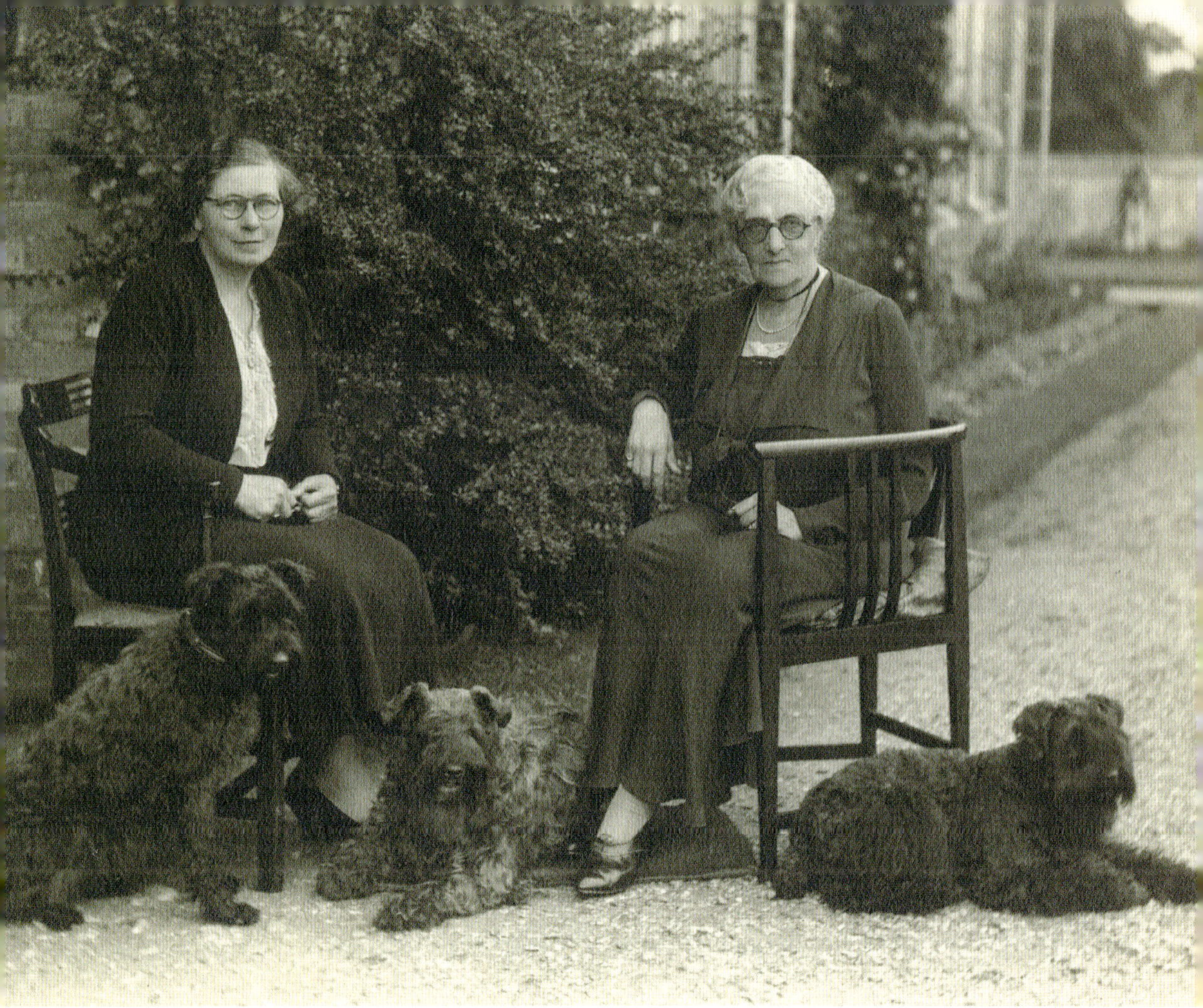

A dog can't think that much about what he's doing, he just does what feels right.

*Barbara Kingsolver, novelist and poet*

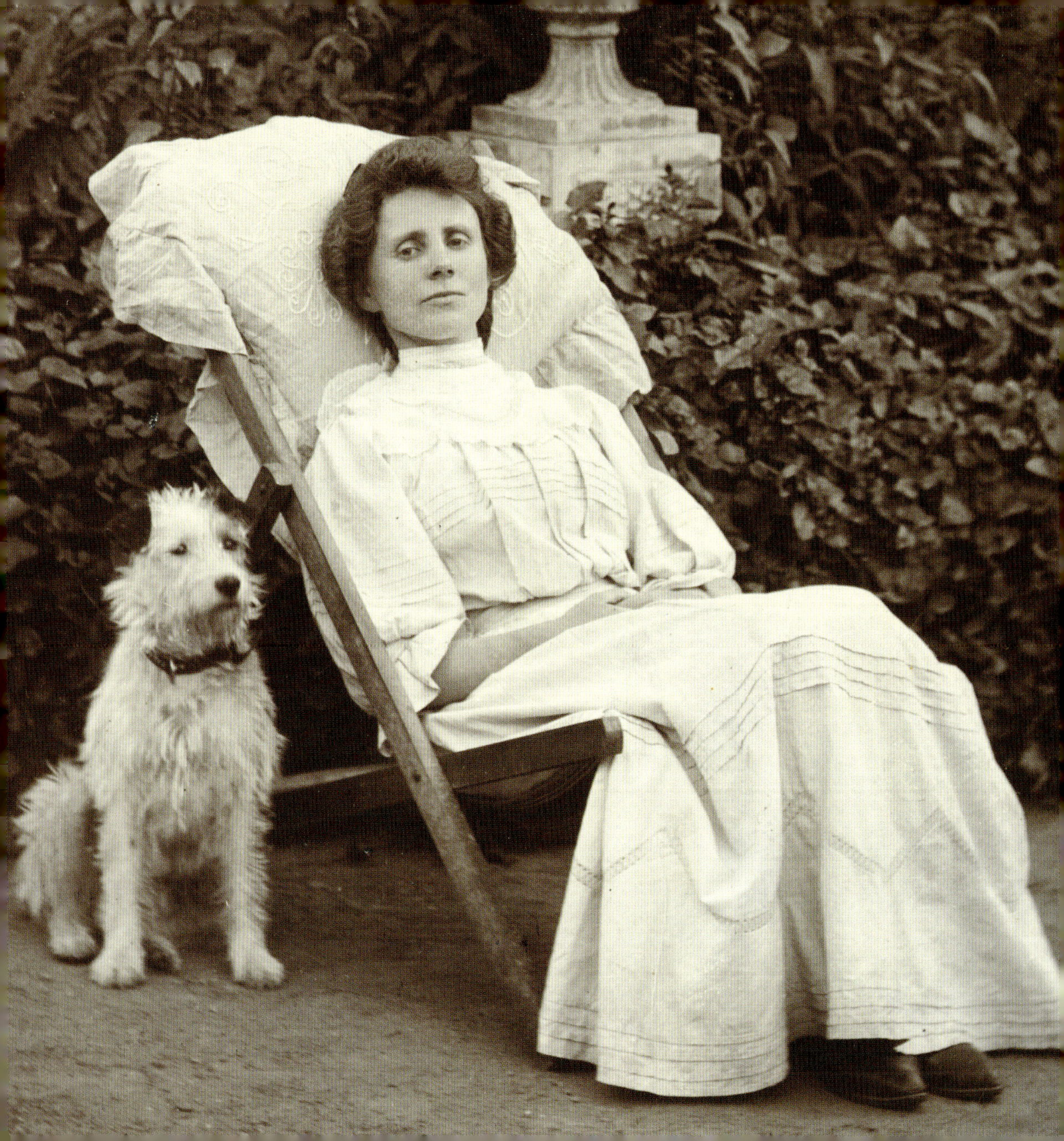

Histories are more full of examples of the fidelity of dogs than of friends.

*Alexander Pope*

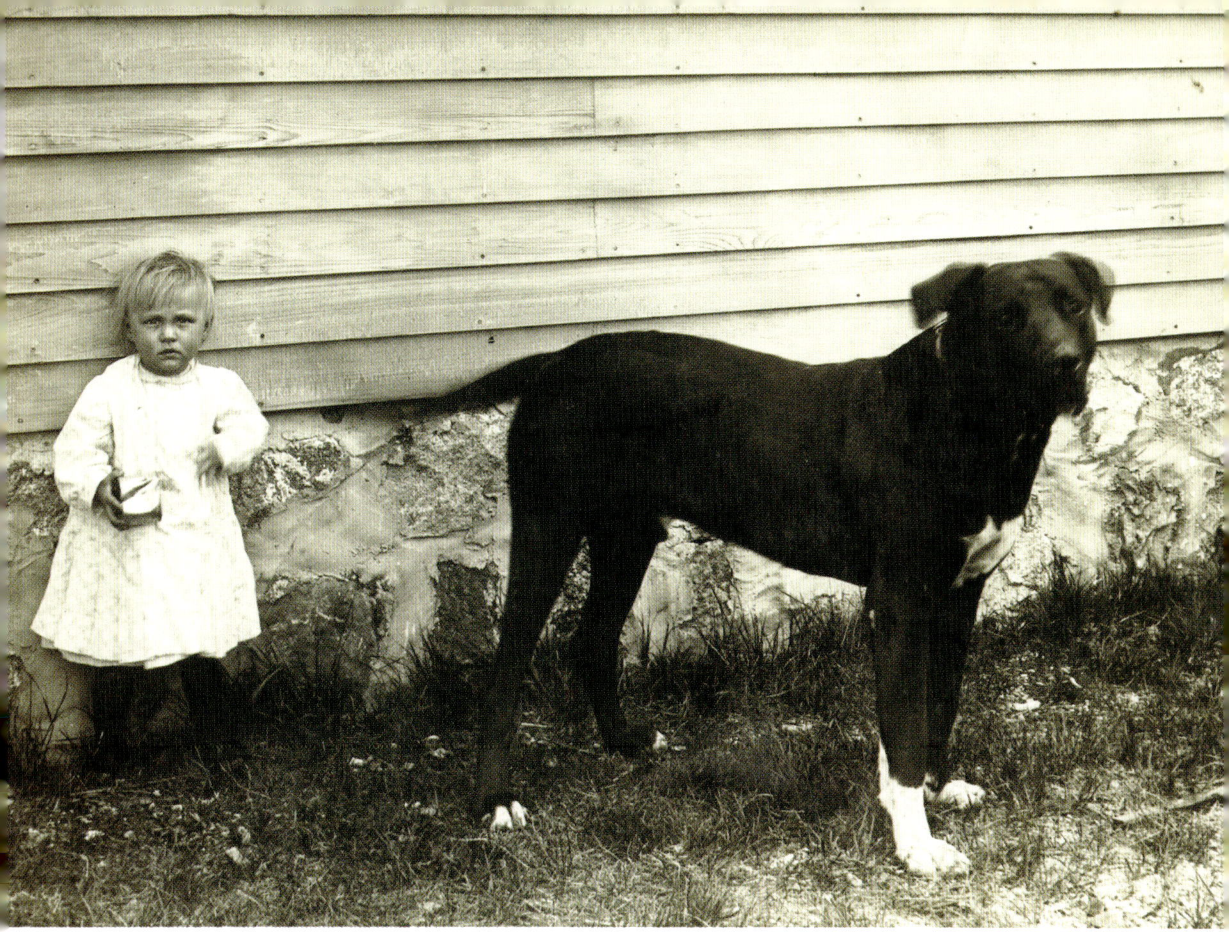

His friends he loved.
His direst earthly foe—Cats—I believe he did but feign to hate.
My hand will miss the insinuated nose,
Mine eyes the tail that wagged contempt at Fate.

*Sir William Watson, poet*

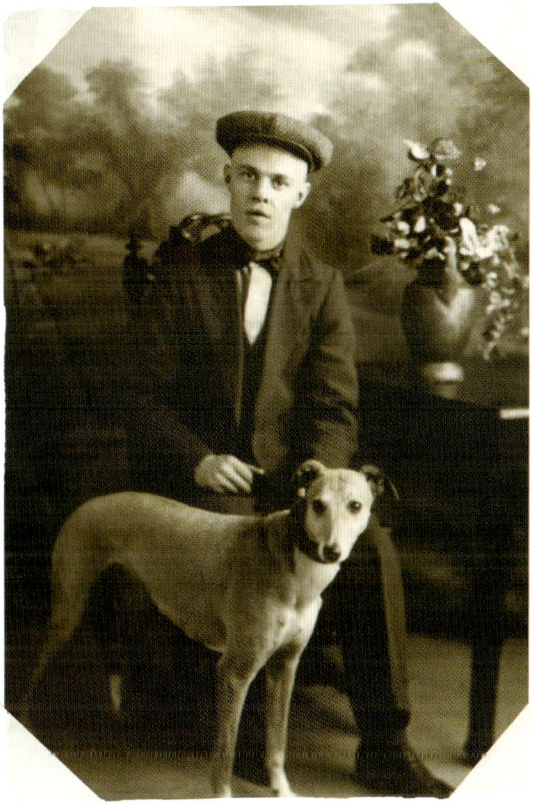

Every dog has his day, unless he loses his tail, then he has a weak-end.

*June Carter Cash, singer*

What joy to watch in lower creature,
Such dawning of a moral nature,
And how (the rule all things obey),
They look to higher mind to be their law
and stay.

*'Sir Walter Scott and his Dogs' by Arthur Henry Hallam, 1893*

---

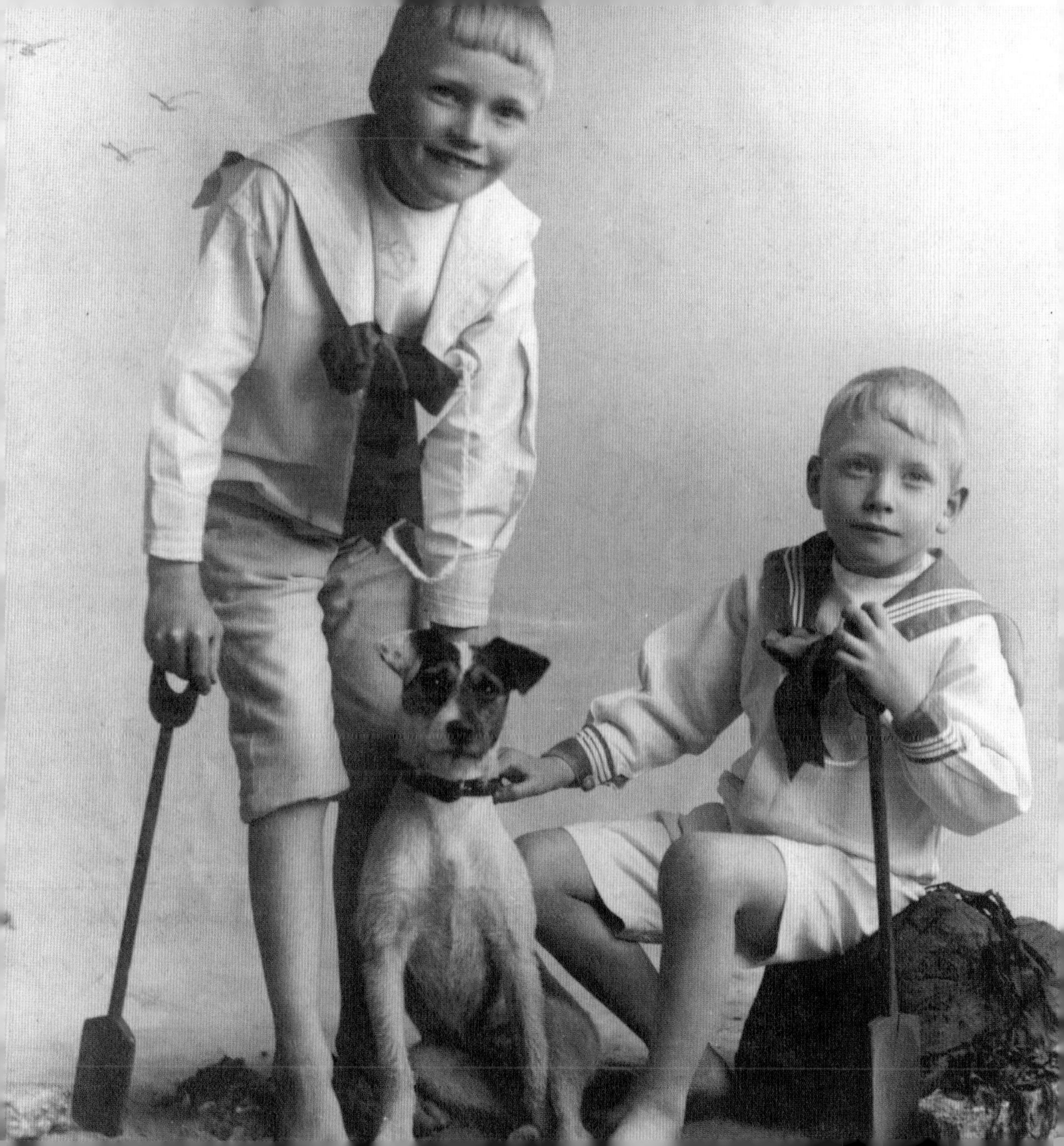

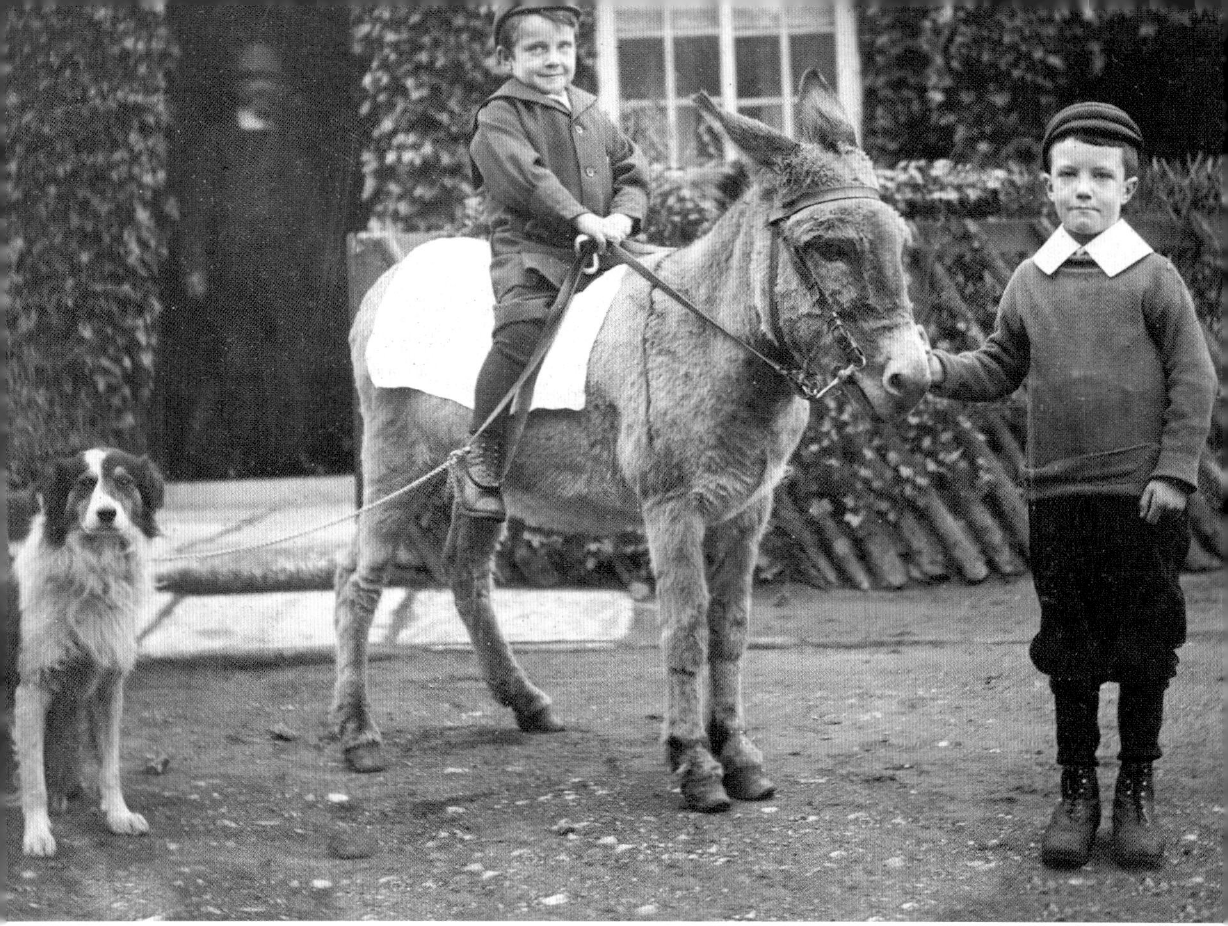

I've seen a look in dogs' eyes, a quickly vanishing look of amazed contempt, and I am convinced that basically dogs think humans are nuts.

*John Steinbeck, author*

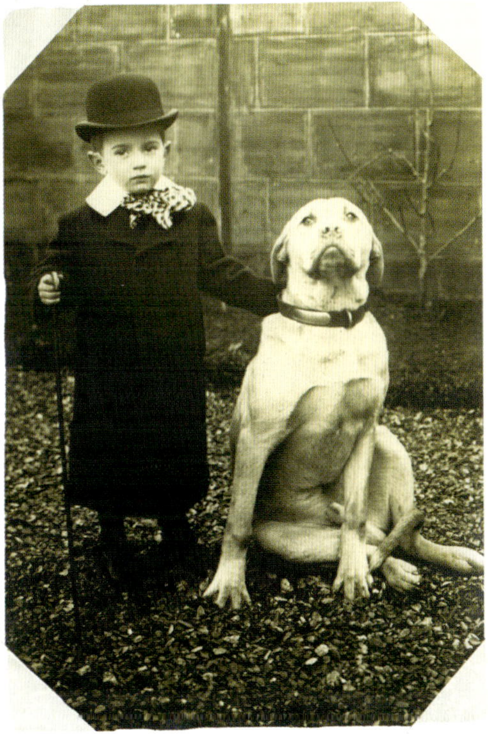

In life the firmest friend,
The first to welcome, foremost to defend,
Whose honest heart is still his master's own,
Who labours, fights, lives, breathes for him alone;

*Lord Byron, poet*

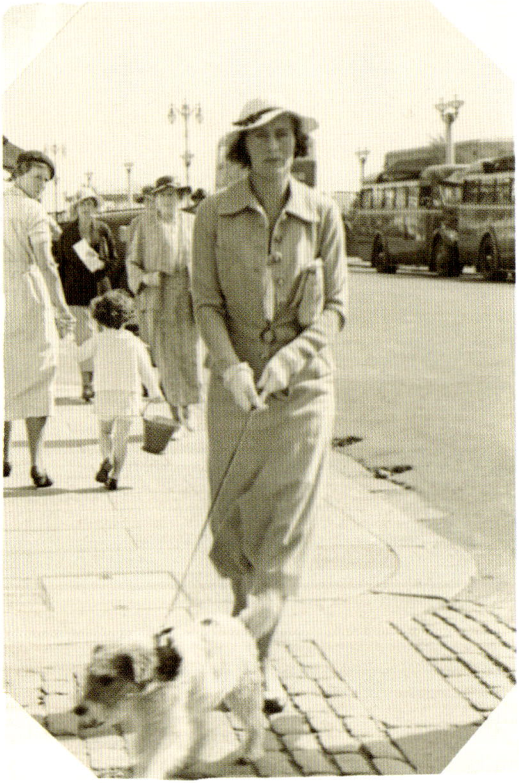

To follow for ten minutes in the street some swaggering canine cavalier, is to receive a lesson in dramatic art and the cultured conduct of the body... All these little gentlemen are subtle casuists... I have called him (Coolin) a snob; but all dogs are so, though in varying degrees...

*Robert Louis Stevenson,*
*novelist and poet*

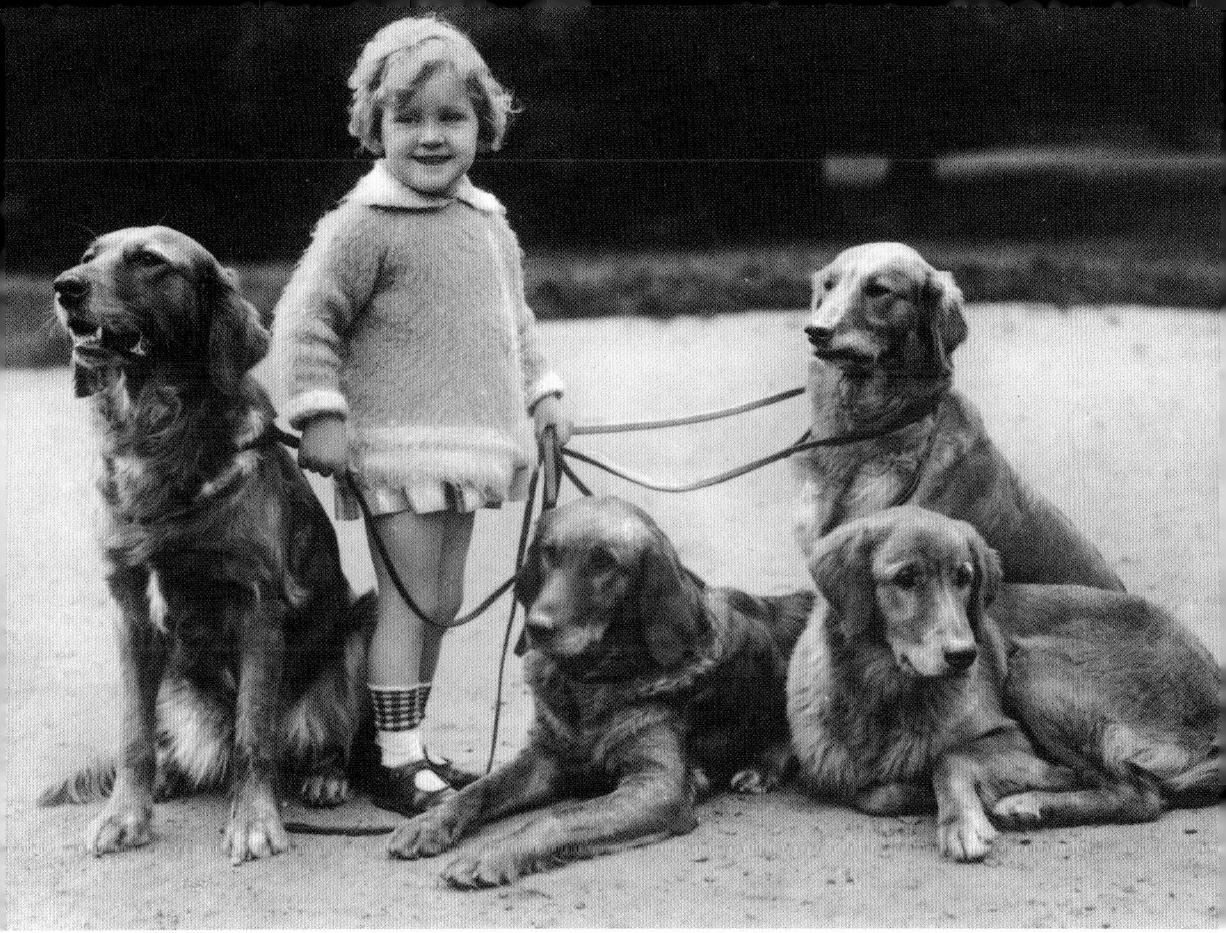

Dogs love their friends and bite their enemies, quite unlike people, who are incapable of pure love and always have to mix love and hate.

*Sigmund Freud, psychoanalyst*

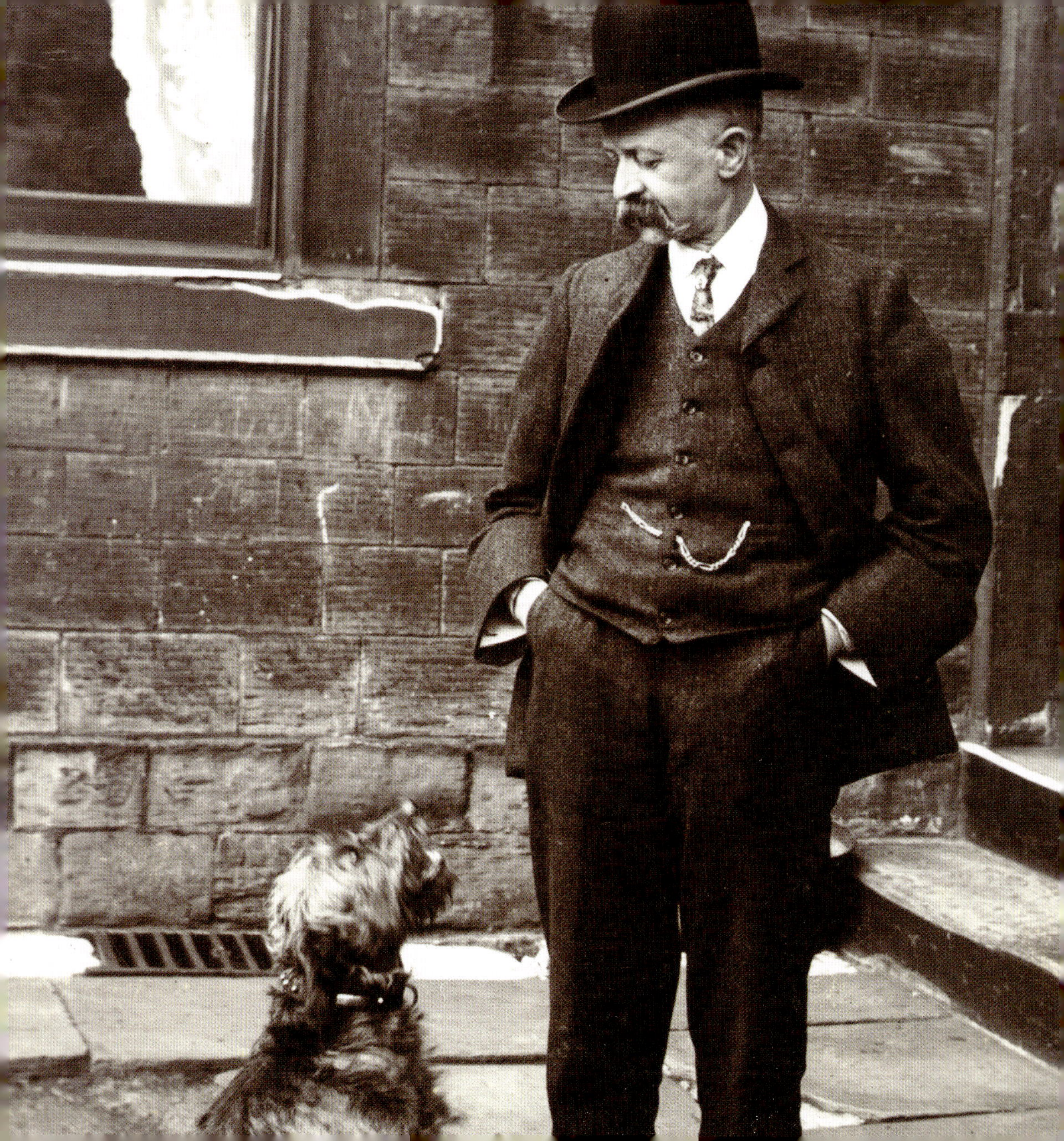

If you want a friend in Washington,
get a dog.

*Harry S. Truman, 33rd President of the United States*

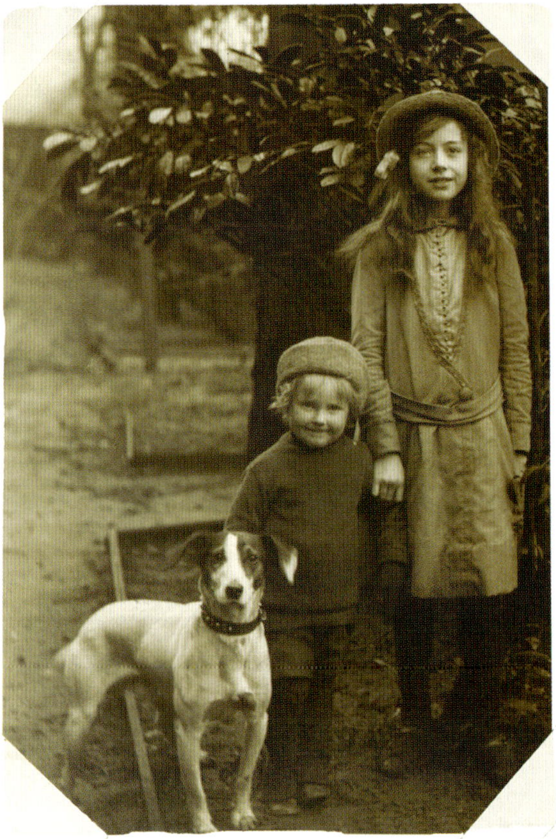

Dogs are wise. They crawl away into a quiet corner and lick their wounds and do not re-join the world until they are whole once more.

*Agatha Christie,*
*author and playwright*

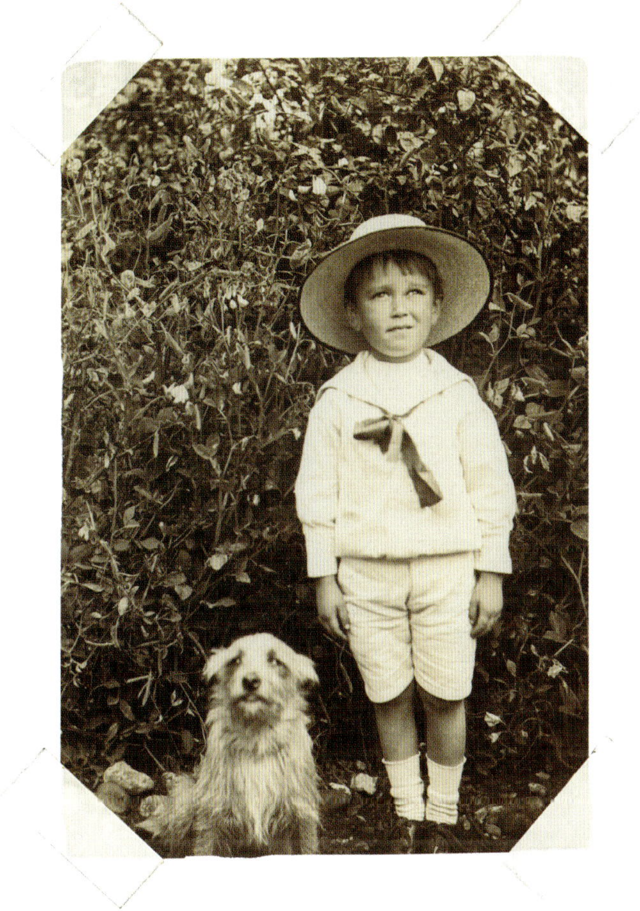

I am not your dog, but if every time you saw me, you gave me a backrub,
I would run to greet you, too.

*Robert Brault, author*

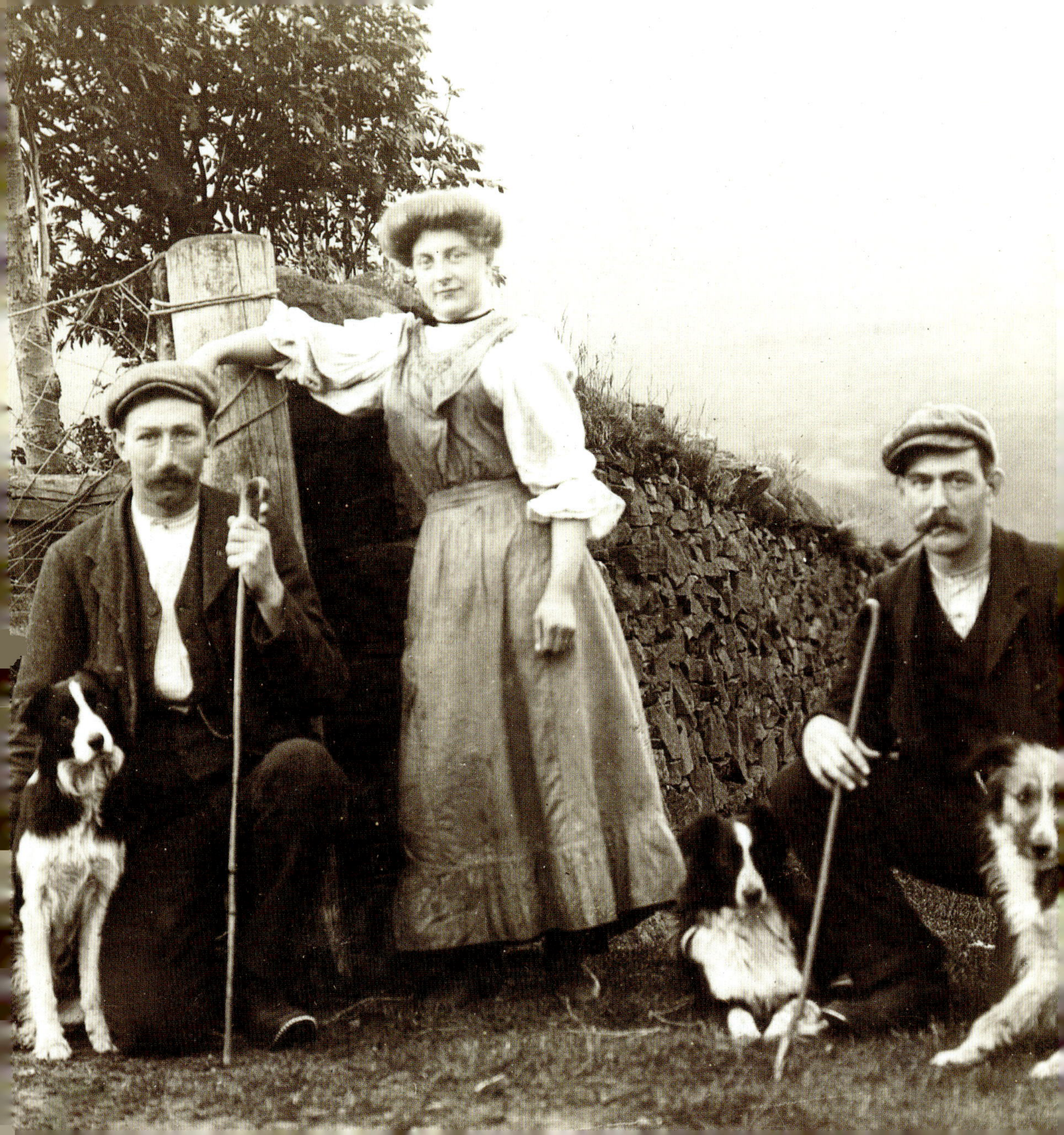

Women and cats will do as they please,
and men and dogs should relax
and get used to the idea.

*Robert A. Heinlein, author*

Hounds follow those who feed them.

*Otto von Bismarck, 1st Chancellor of Germany*

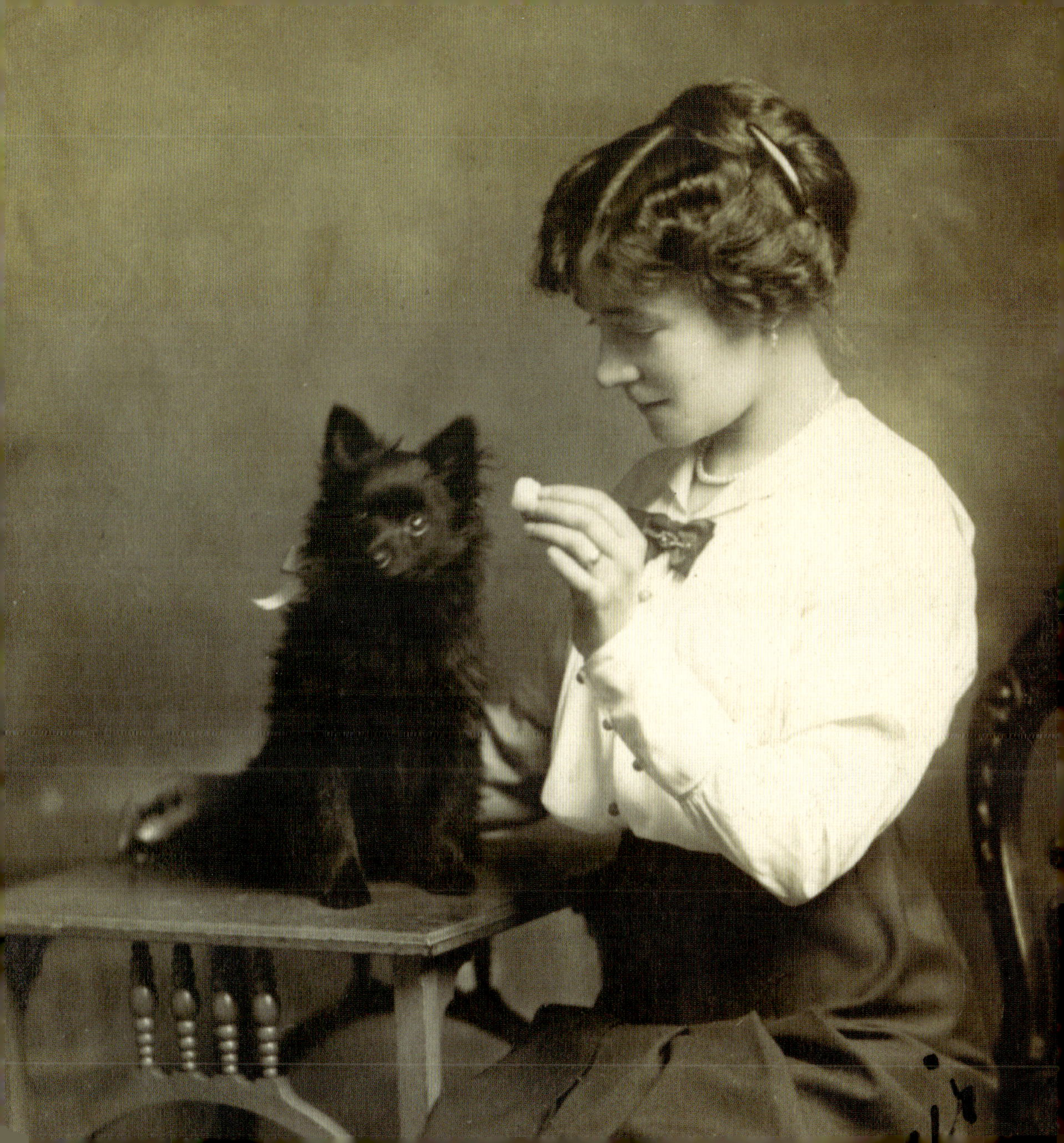

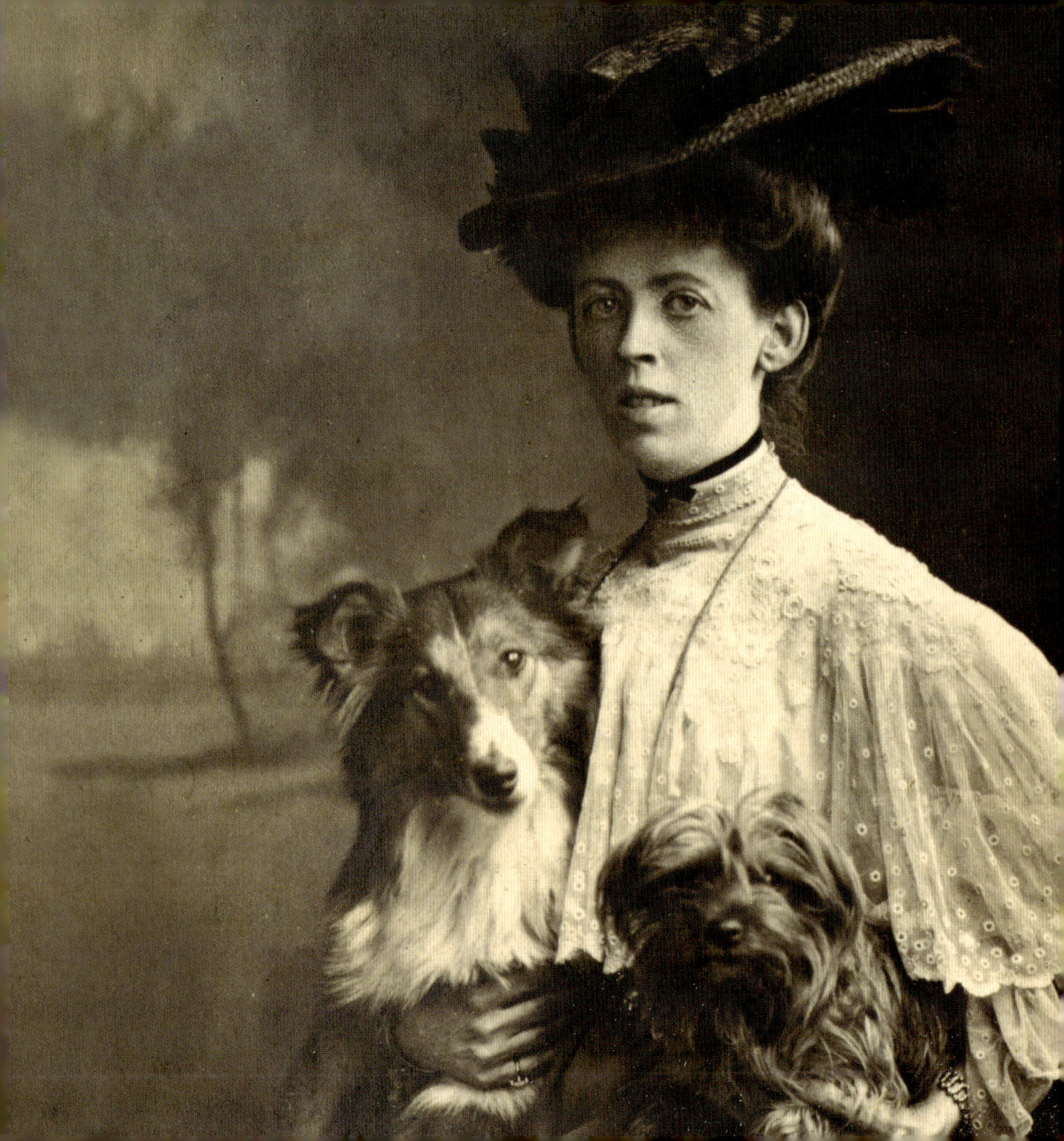

It's not the size of the dog in the fight, it's the size of the fight in the dog.

*attributed to Mark Twain and various others*

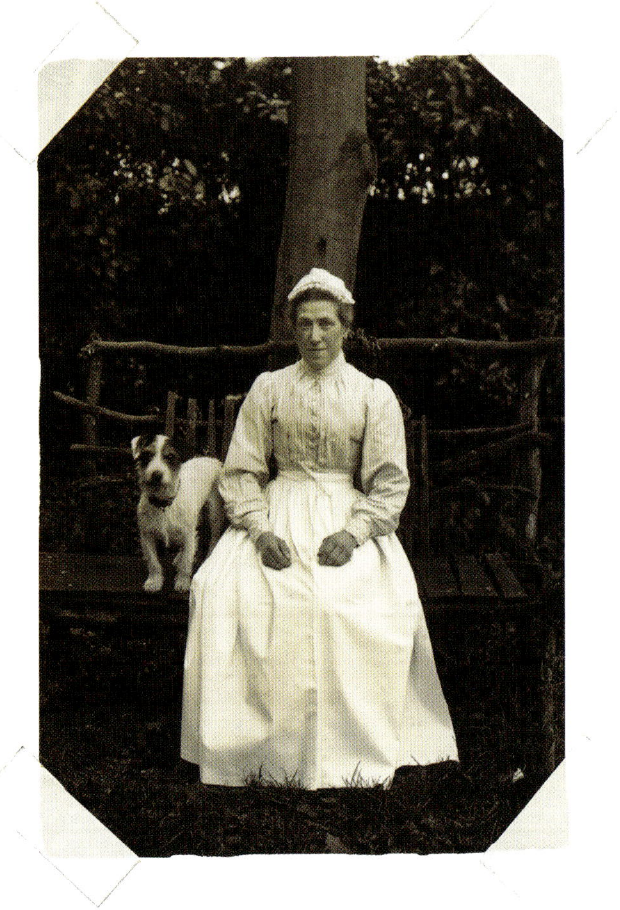

No one appreciates the very special genius of your conversation as the dog does.

*Christopher Morley, author*

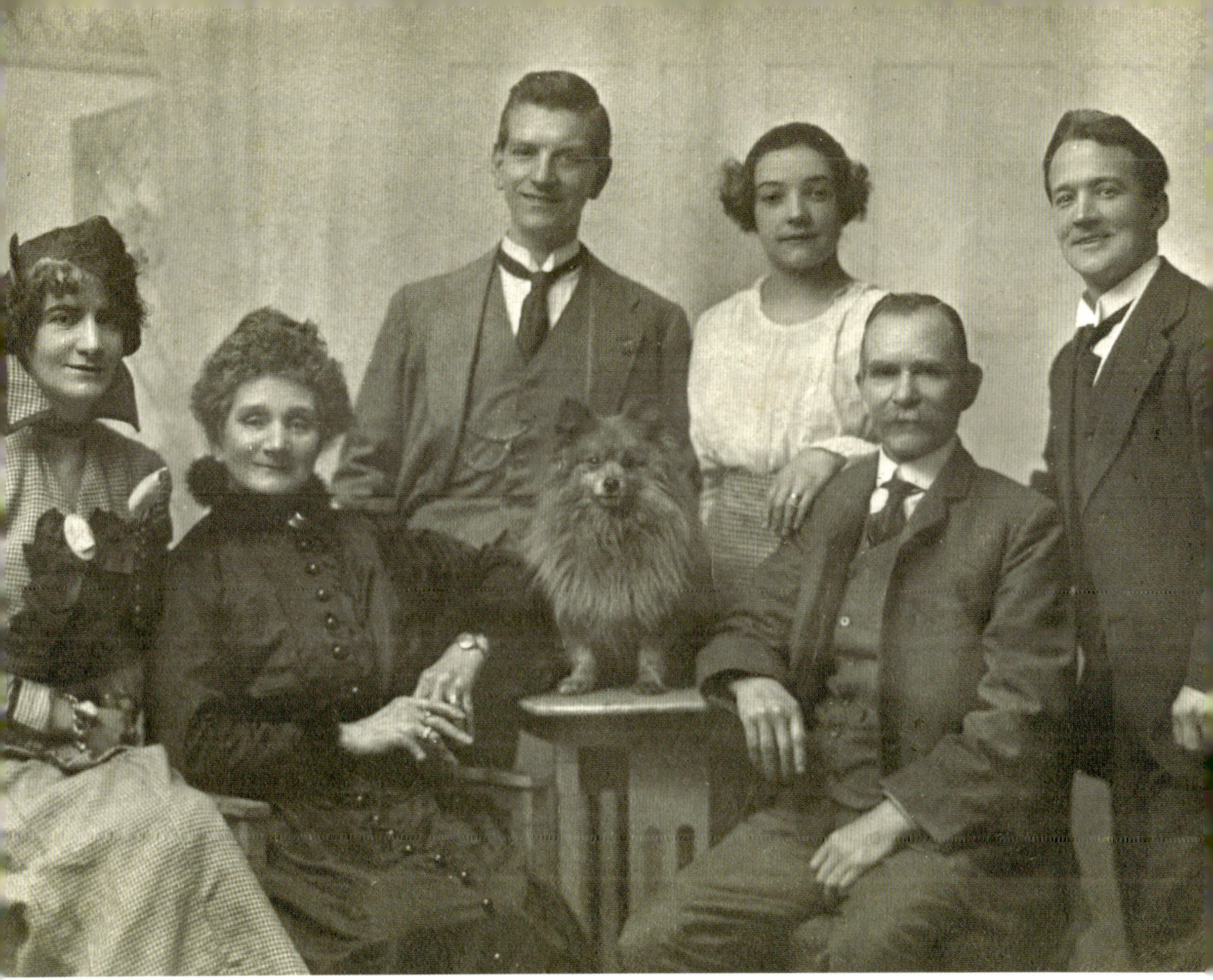

Our dogs will love and admire the meanest of us, and feed our colossal vanity with their uncritical homage.

*Agnes Repplier, essayist*

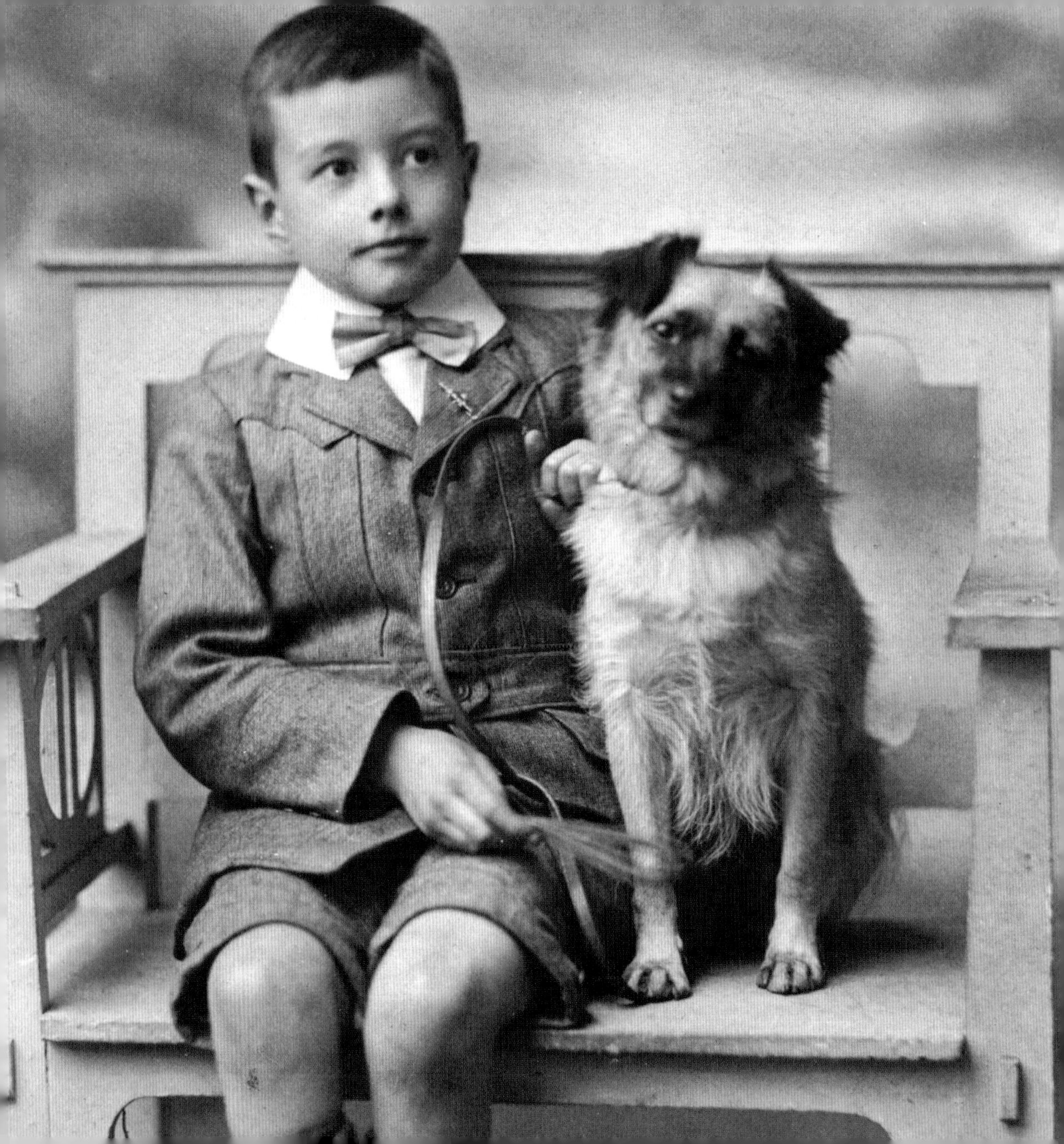

The dog whom nothing can mislead
must be a dog of parts indeed.
Is often wiser than his master.

*Somerville*

My goal in life is to be as good of a person my dog already thinks I am.

*Author unknown*

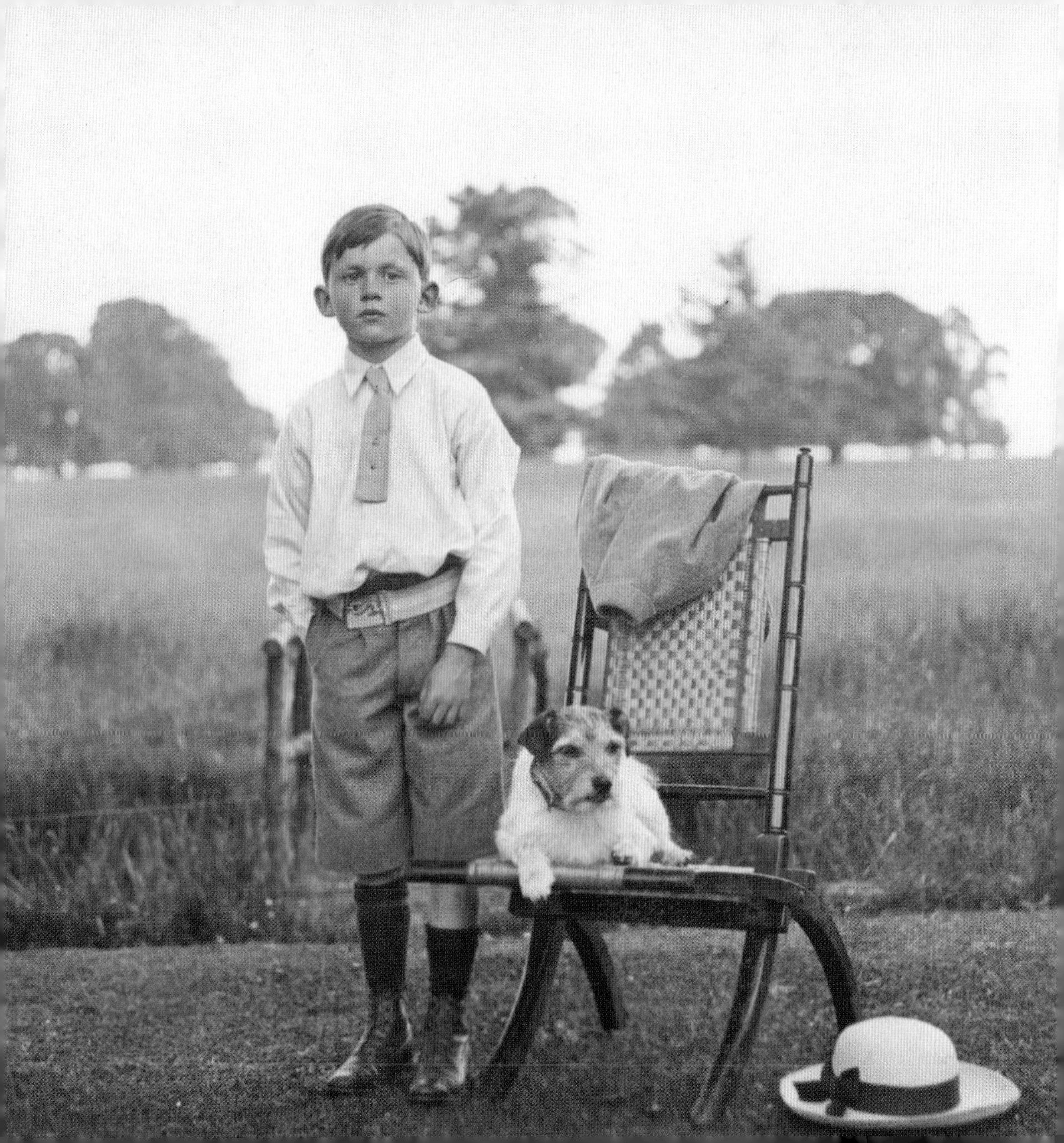

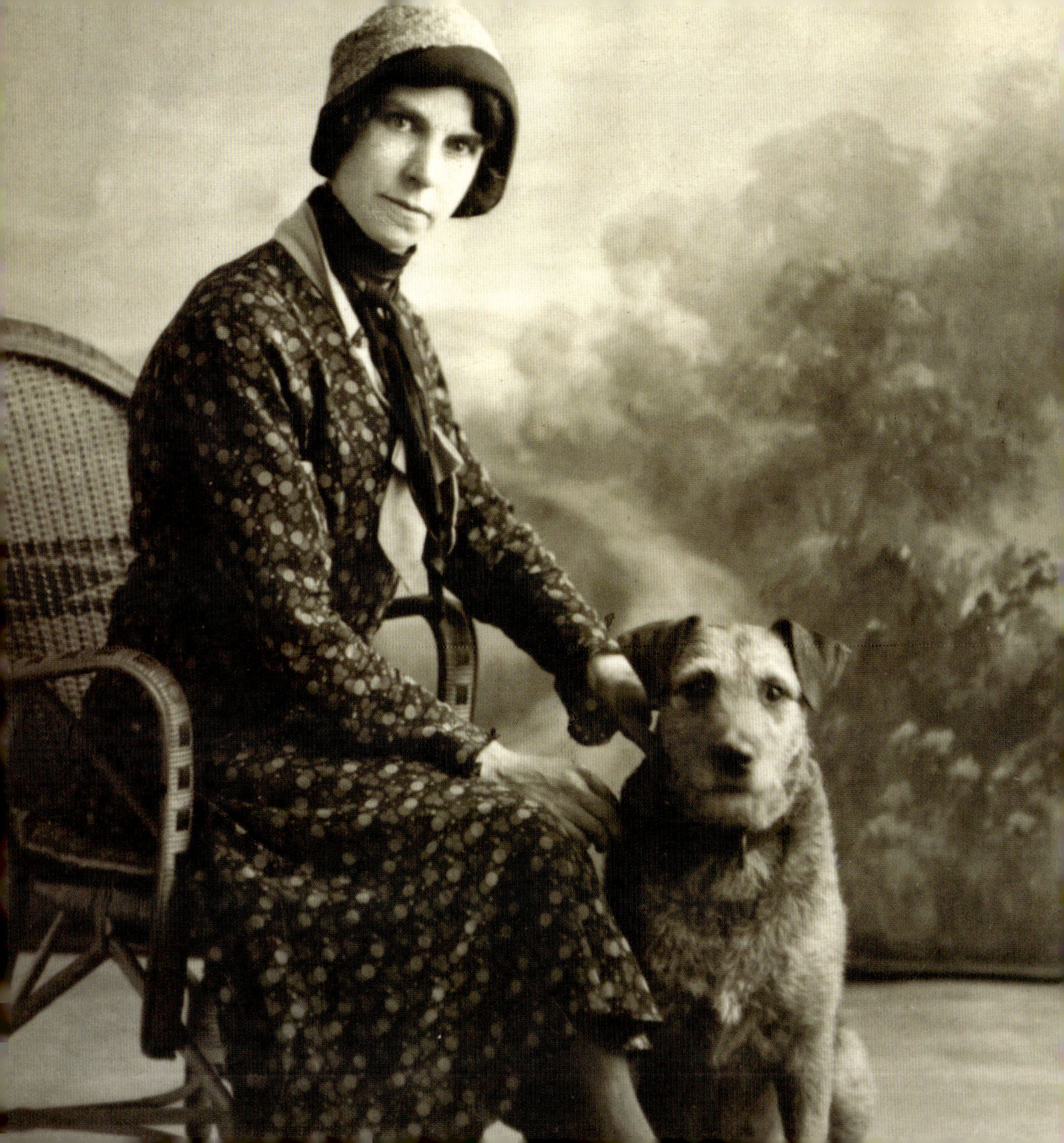

Dogs have been known to die from excess of joy at seeing their masters after a long absence. An English officer had a large dog, which he left with his family in England, while he accompanied an expedition to America, during the war of the Colonies. Throughout his absence, the animal appeared very much dejected. When the Officer returned home, the dog who happened to be lying at the door of an apartment into which his master was about to enter, immediately recognized him, leapt upon his neck, licked his face, and in a few minutes fell dead at this feet. A favourite spaniel of a lady recently died on seeing his beloved mistress after a long absence.

*Anecdotes of Dogs by Edward Jesse, 1846*

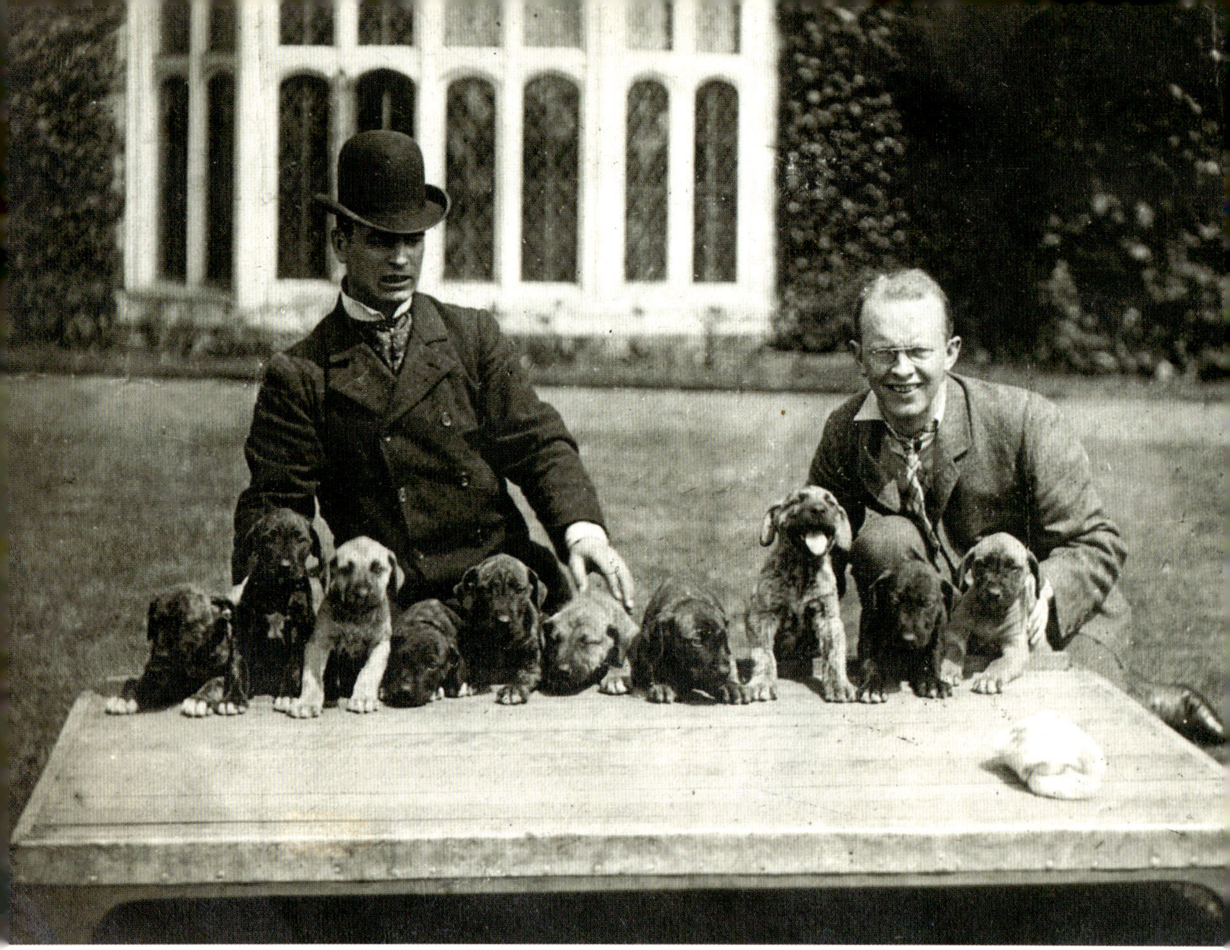

Ever consider what our dogs must think of us? I mean, here we come back from a grocery store with the most amazing haul, chicken, pork, half a cow. They must think we're the greatest hunters on earth!

*Anne Tyler, author*

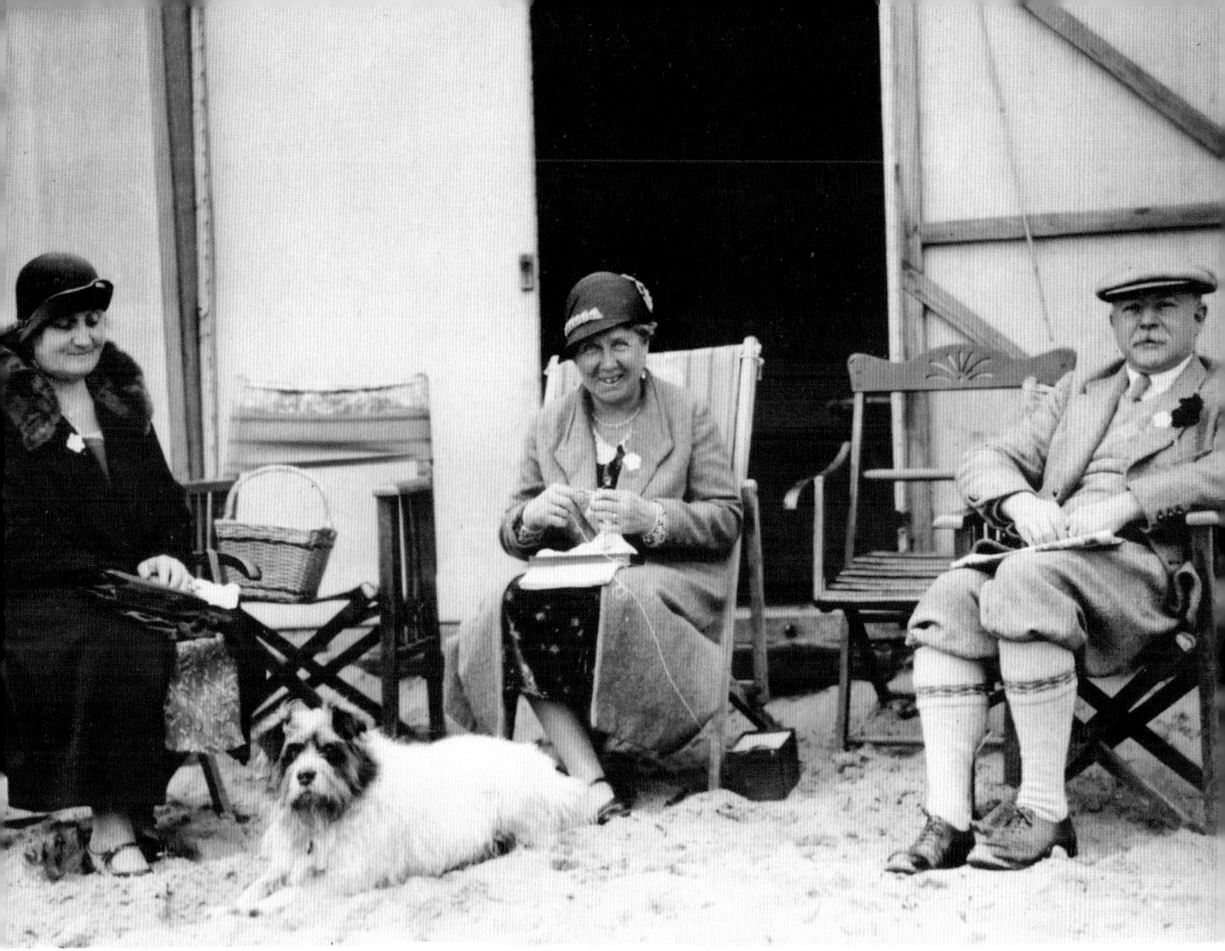

I think we are drawn to dogs because they are the uninhibited creatures we might be if we weren't certain we knew better. They fight for honor at the first challenge, make love with no moral restraint, and they do not for all their marvelous instincts appear to know about death. Being such wonderfully uncomplicated beings, they need us to do their worrying.

*George Bird Evans, Troubles with Bird Dogs*

Man is a dog's idea of what
God should be.

*Holbrook Jackson, journalist and publisher*

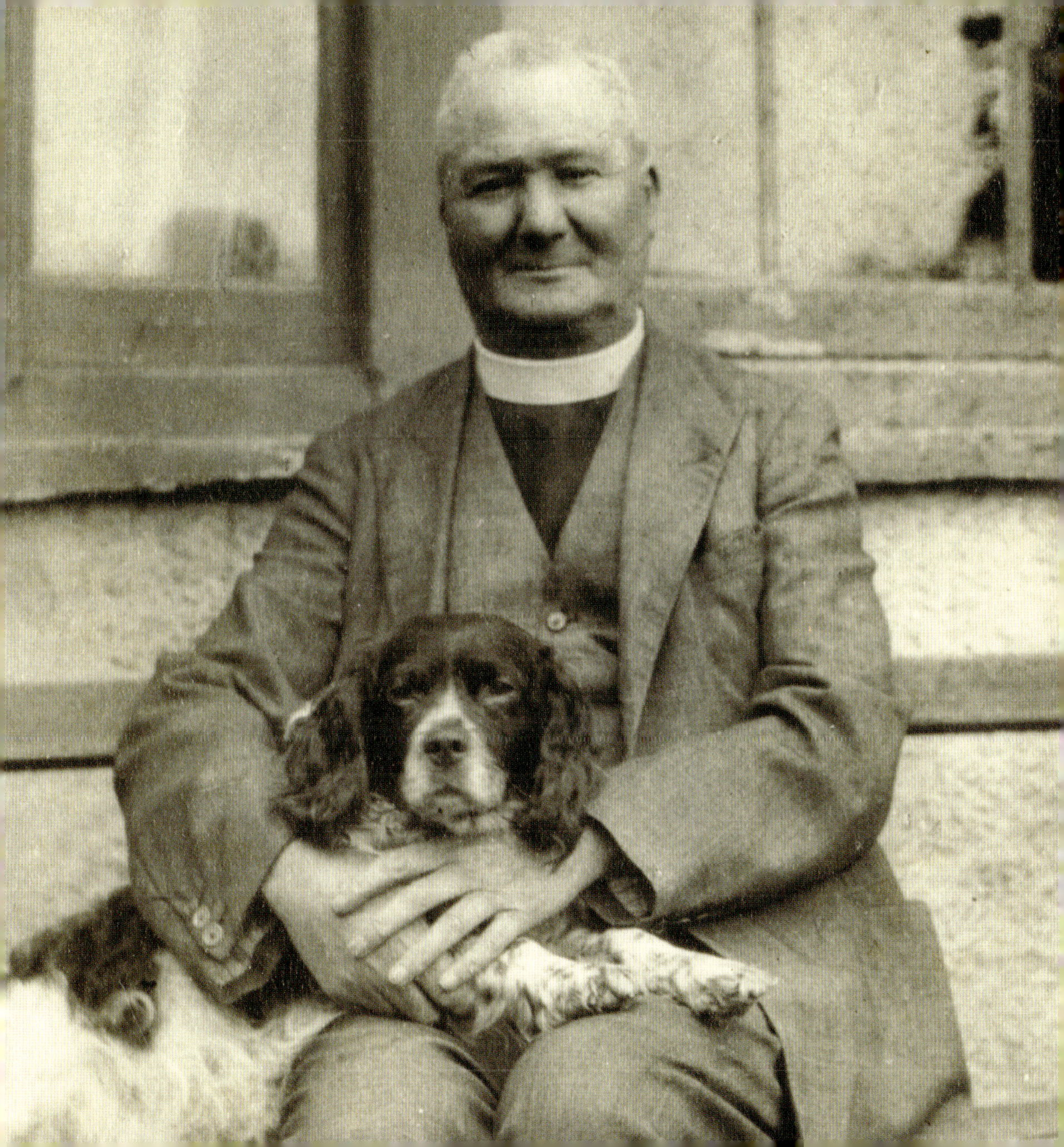

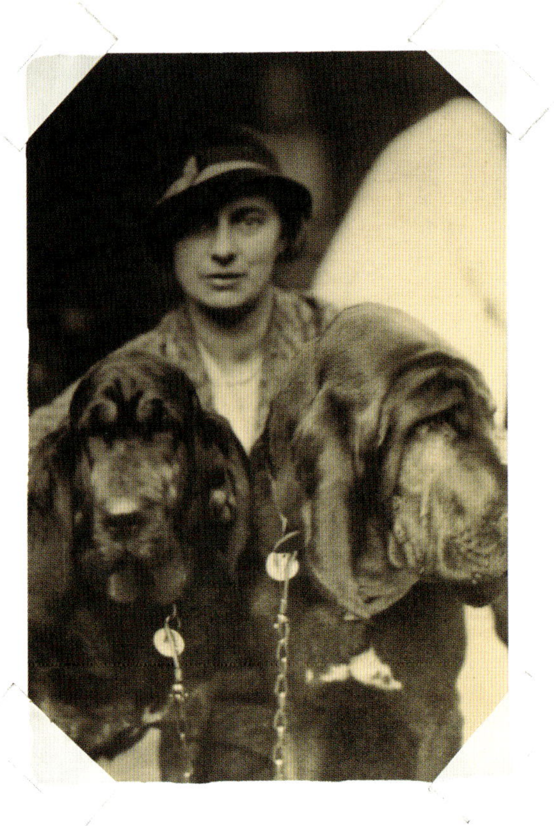

A dog is not "almost human" and I know of no greater insult to the canine race than to describe it as such.

*John Holmes, author*

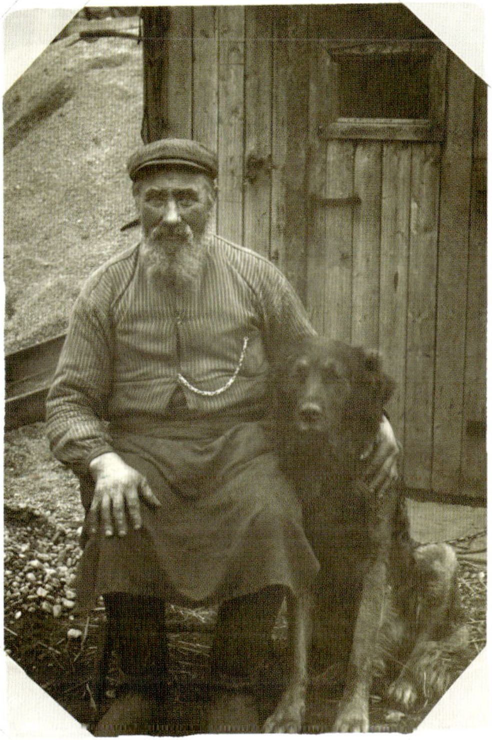

Dogs' lives are too short.
Their only fault, really.

*Agnes Sligh Turnbull, writer*

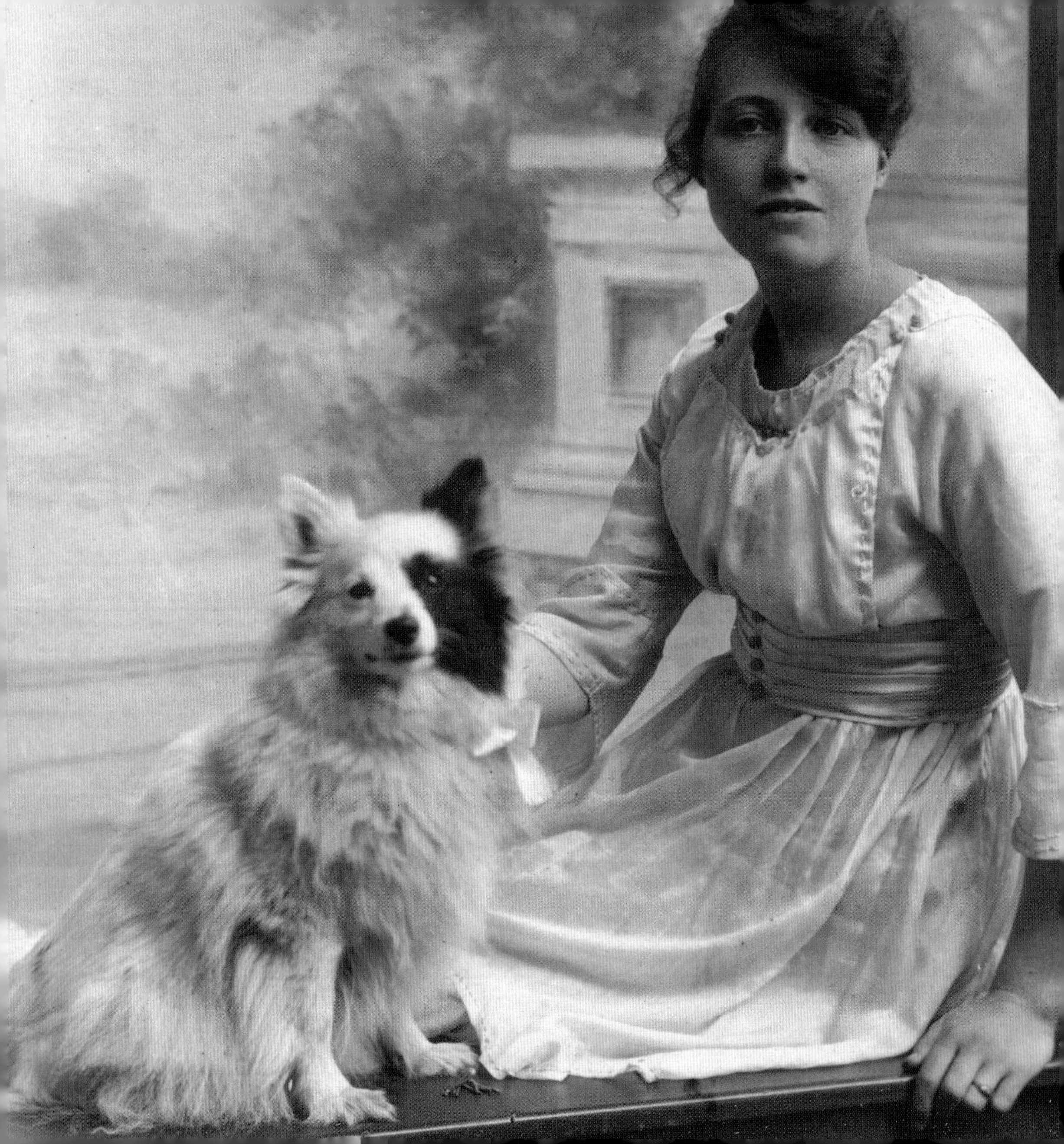

The reason a dog has so many friends is that he wags his tail instead of his tongue.

*Author unknown*

He makes us feel that his dogs will love us without selfishness, and defend us at the risk of their own lives. That though friends may forsake us, they never will—and that in misfortune, poverty and death, their affection will be unchanged, and their gratitude unceasing.'

*Sir Edwin Landseer in 'Anecdotes of Dogs', 1846*

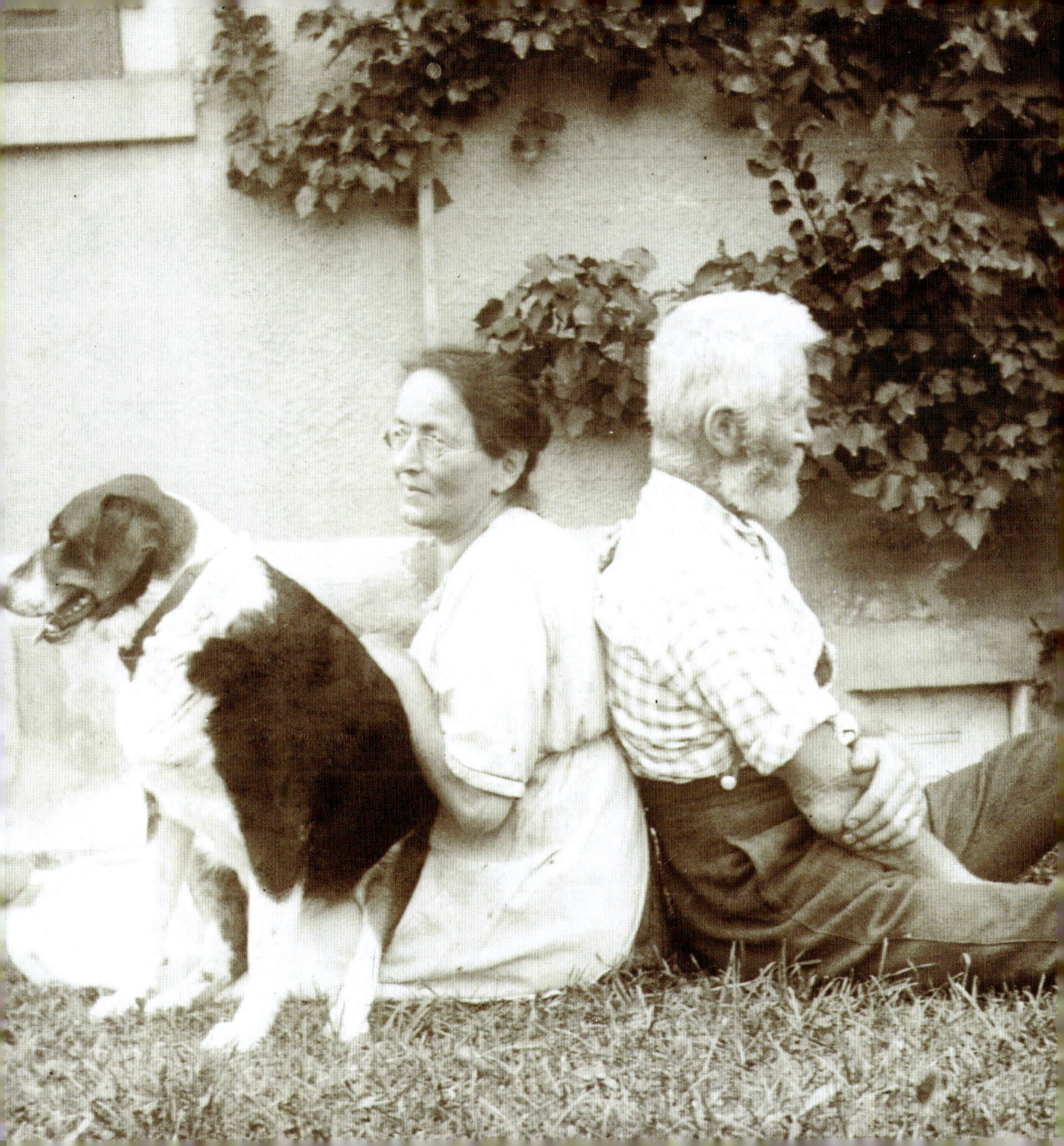

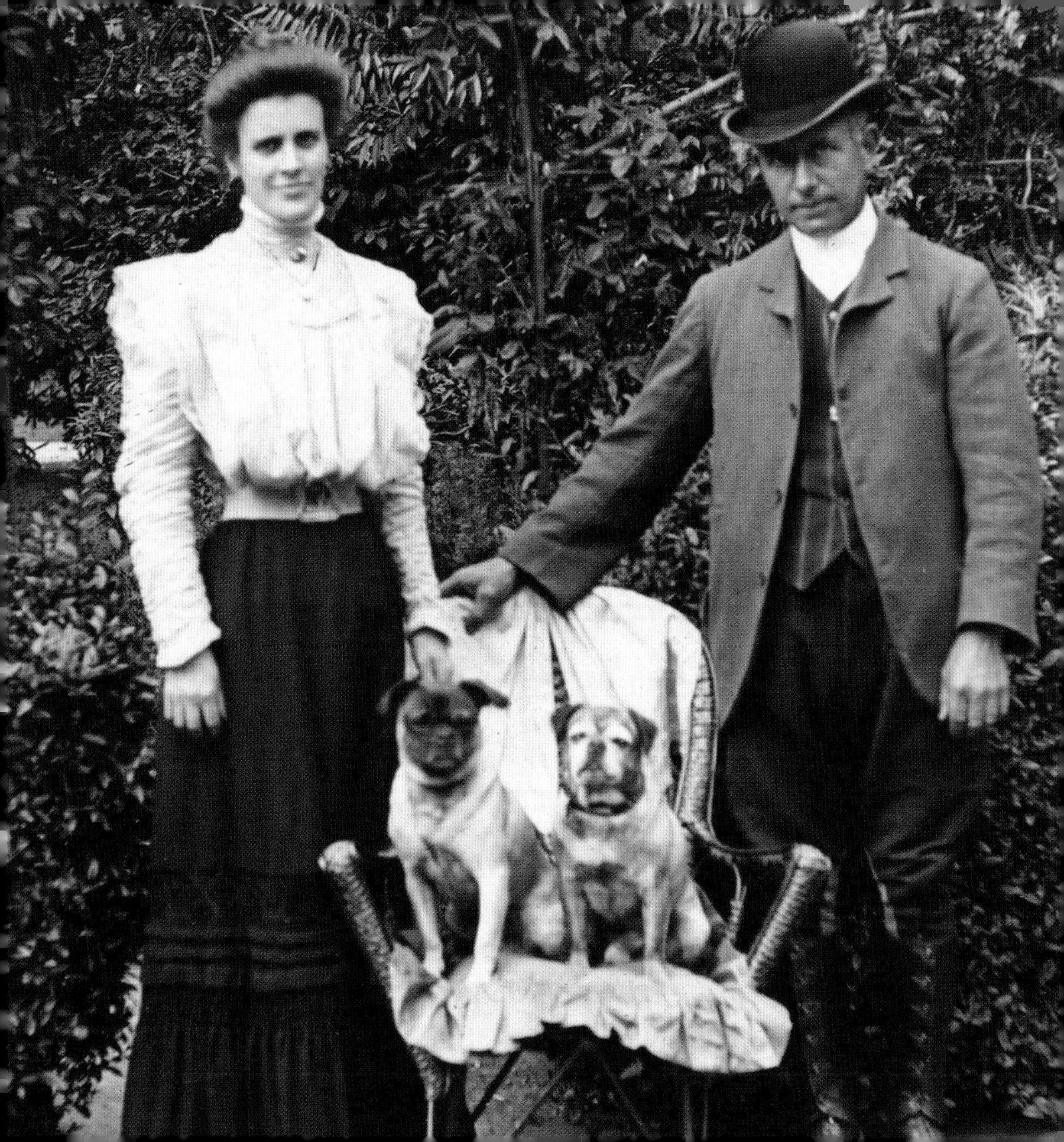

We long for an affection altogether ignorant of our faults. Heaven has accorded this to us in the uncritical canine attachment.

*George Eliot*

*(aka Mary Ann Evans),*

*journalist and writer*

My little dog—a heartbeat at my feet.

*Edith Wharton*

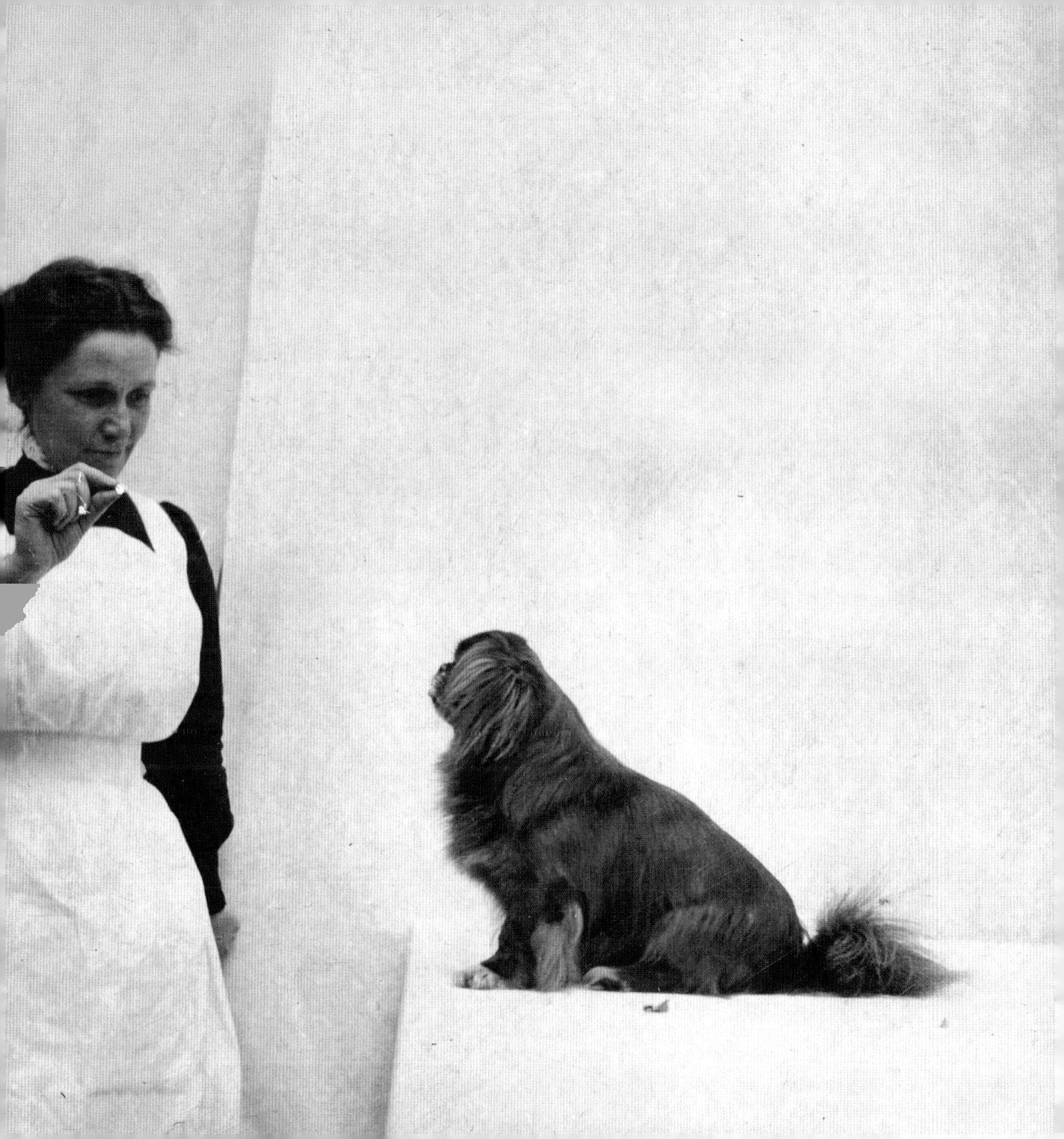

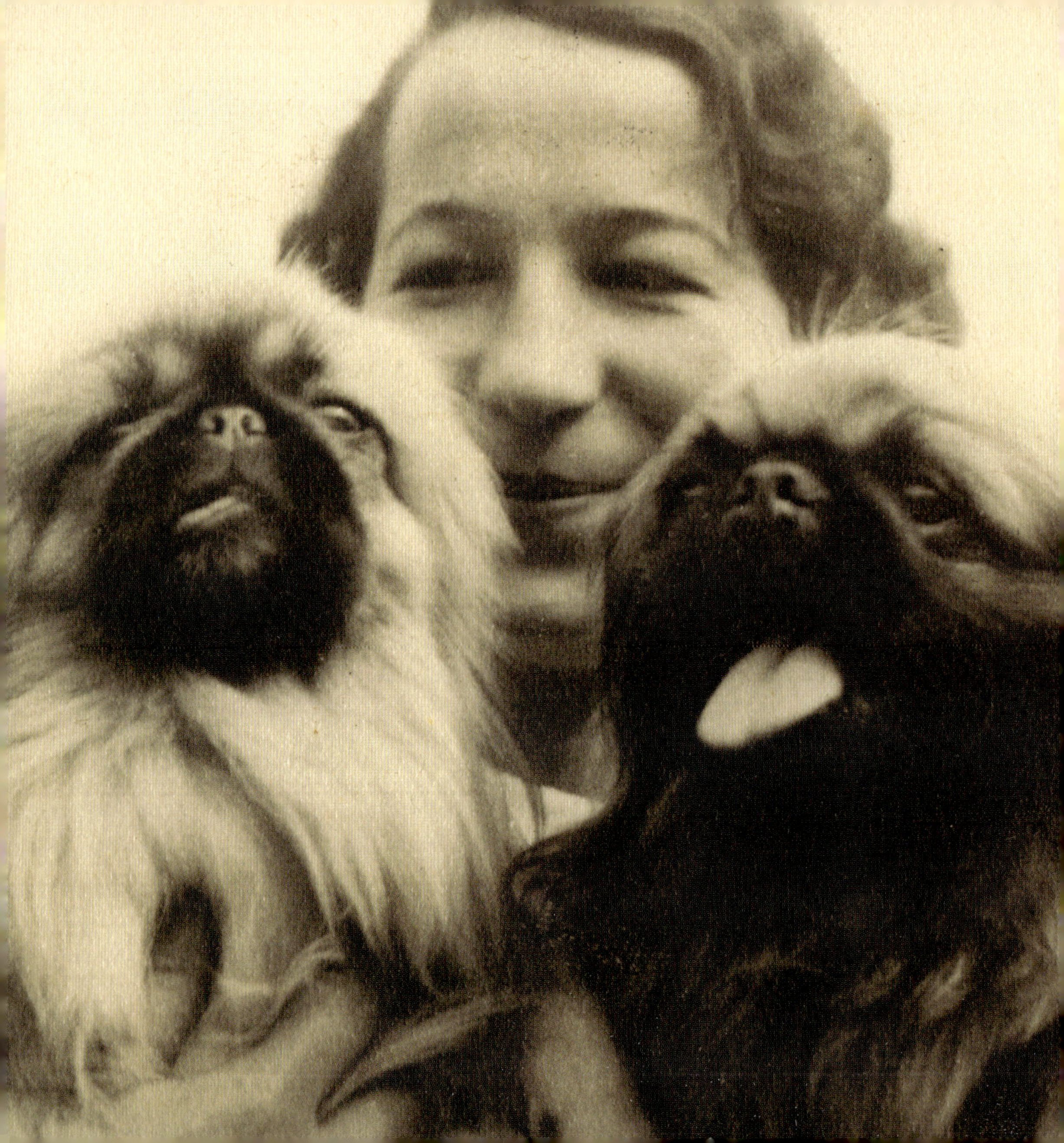

There is no psychiatrist in the world like a puppy licking your face.

*Ben Williams,*

*novelist and short story writer*

From the dog's point of view, his master is an elongated and abnormally cunning dog.

*Mabel Louise Robinson, author*

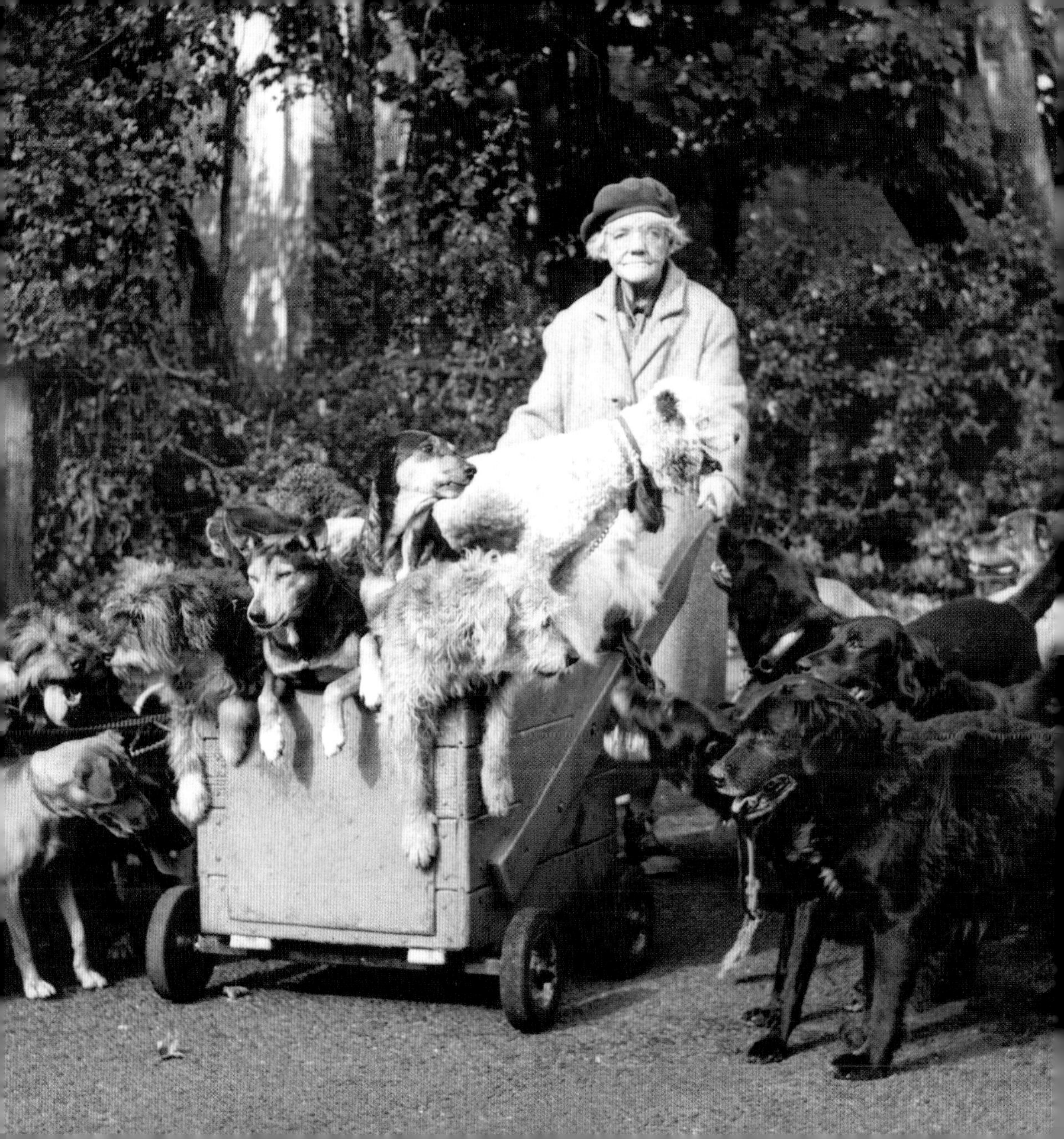

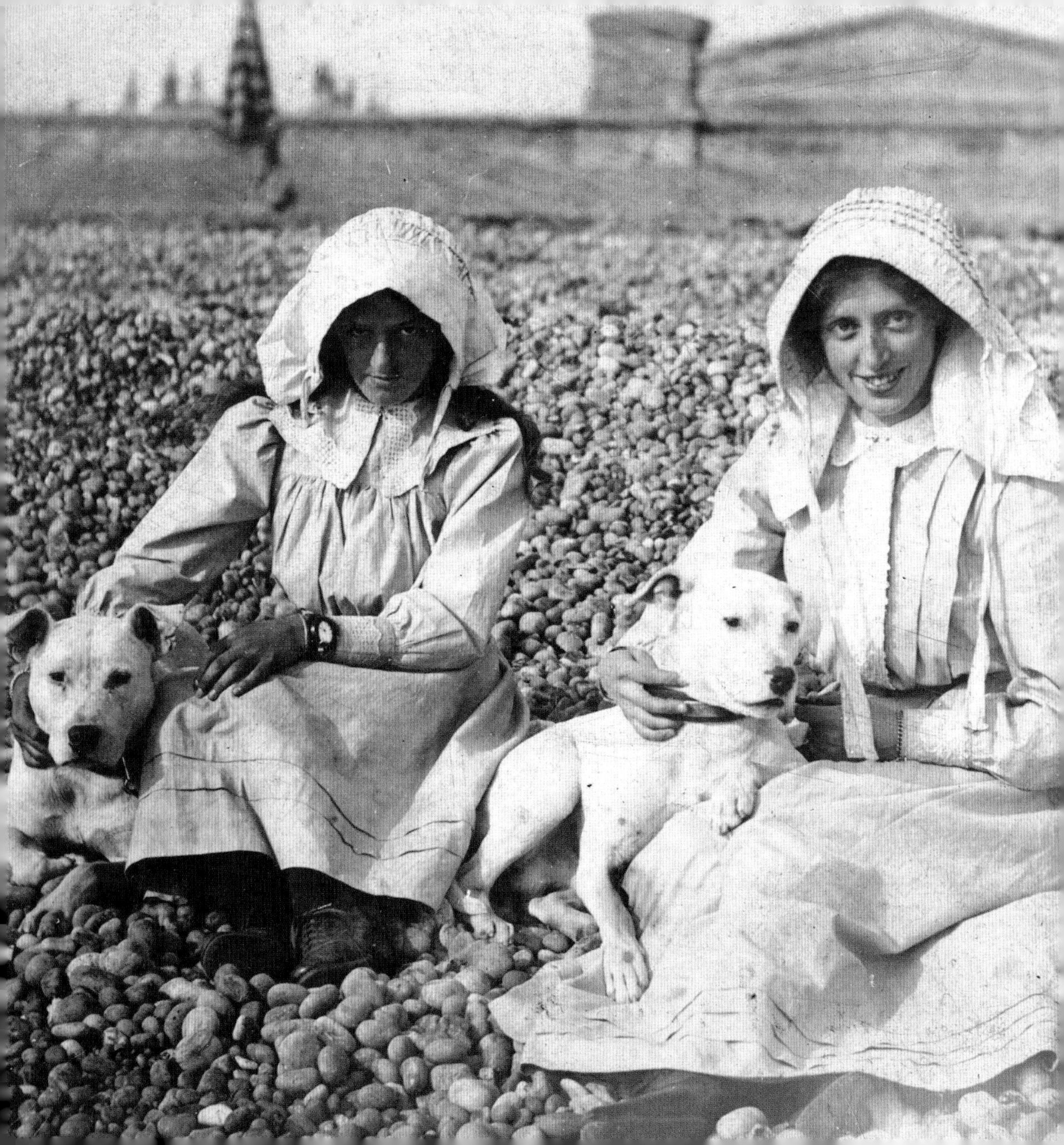

I always like a dog so long as he isn't spelled backward.

*G.K. Chesterton, writer, poet and philosopher*

Why does watching a dog be a dog fill one with happiness?'

*Jonathan Safran Foer, author*

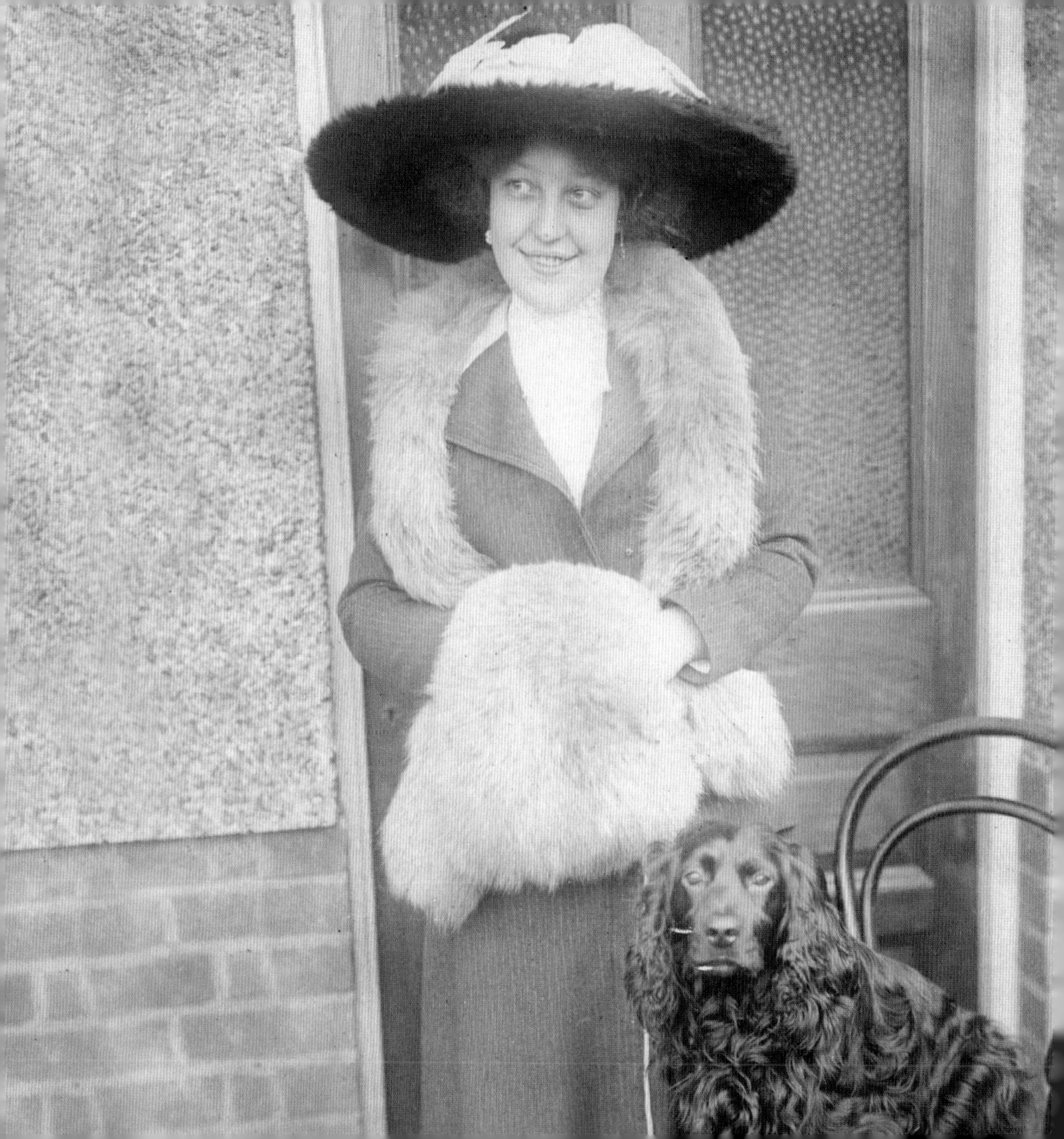

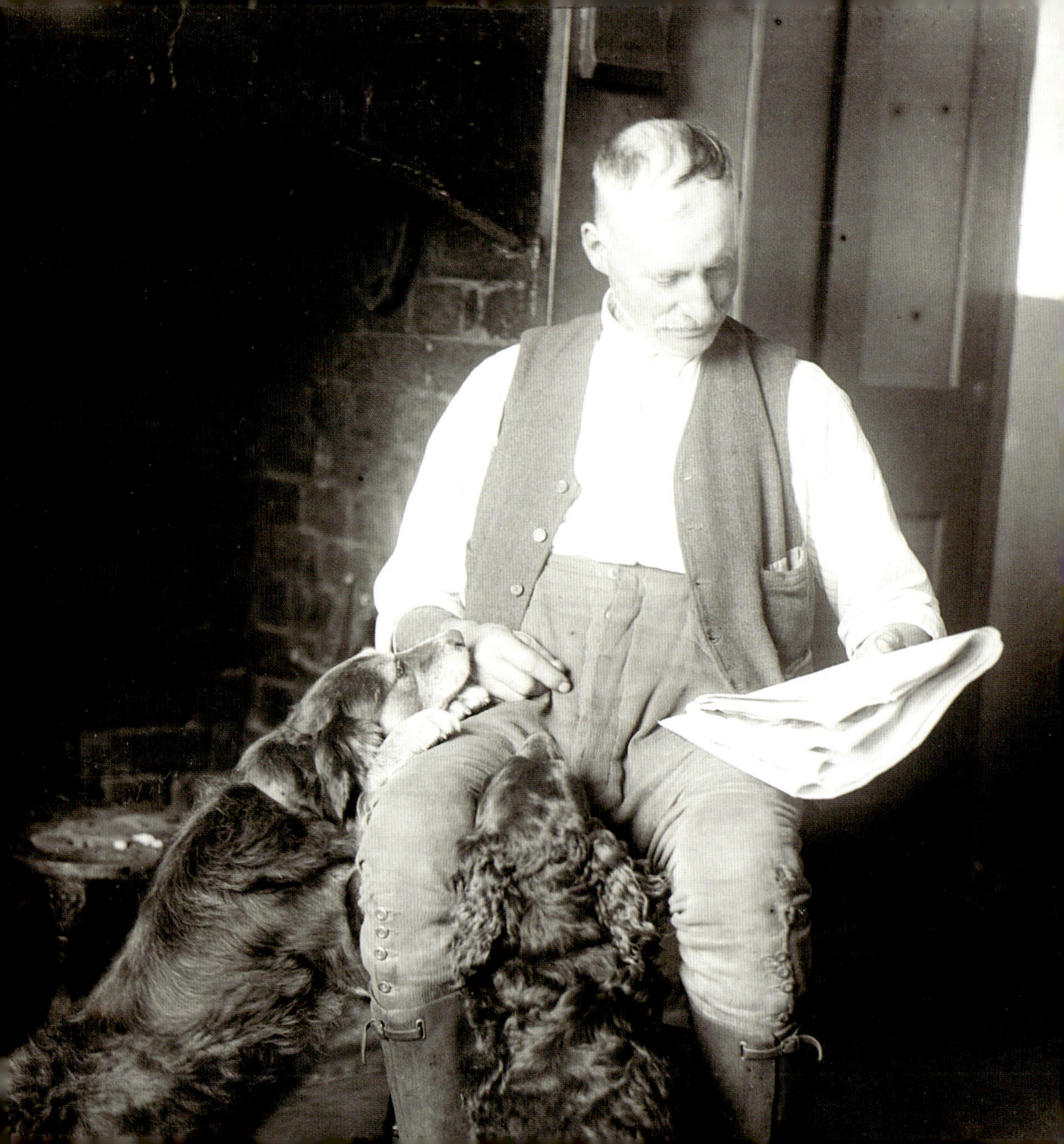

There is a well-known story of a farmer, who returning home, in winter from a market town, while in a state of intoxication, had his life saved by his faithful sheep-dog.
On being afterwards offered a large sum for the animal, he said, that so long as he had a bone to his meat, or a crust to his bread, he would divide it with the faithful friend, who had saved his life.

*Anecdotes of Dogs by Edward Jesse, 1846*

---

Dachshunds are ideal dogs for small children, as they are already stretched and pulled to such a length that a child cannot do much harm one way or another.

*Robert Benchley*

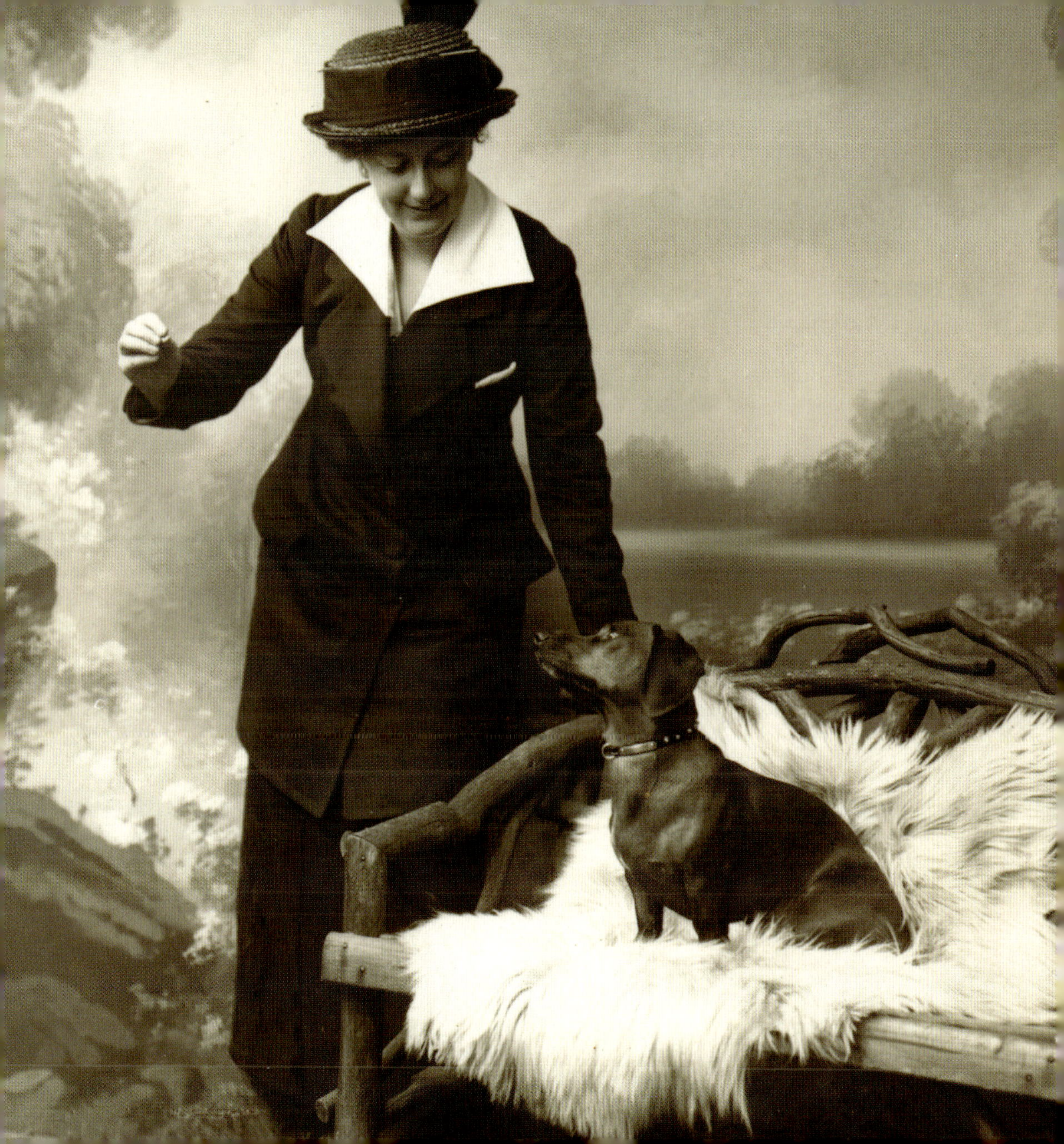

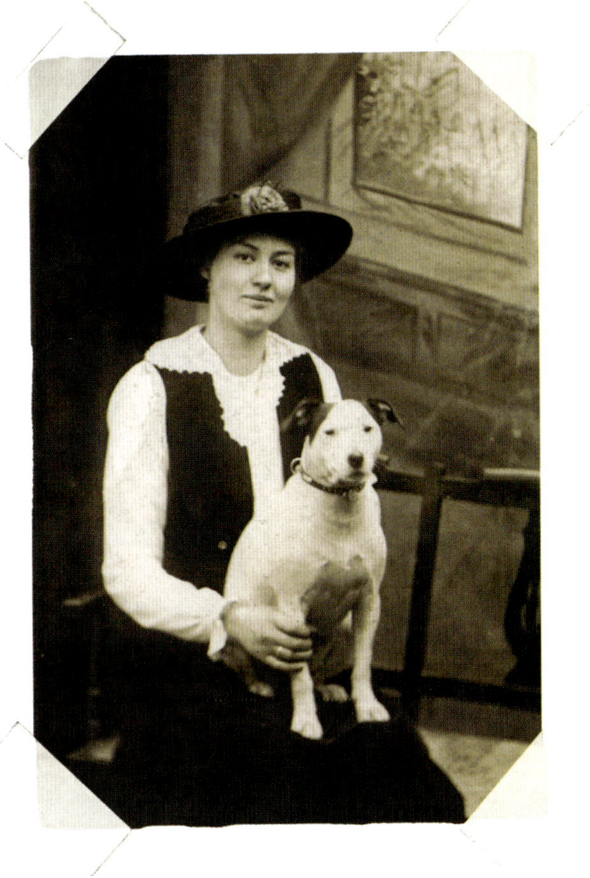

One reason a dog can be such a comfort when you're feeling blue is that he doesn't try to find out why.

*Author unknown*

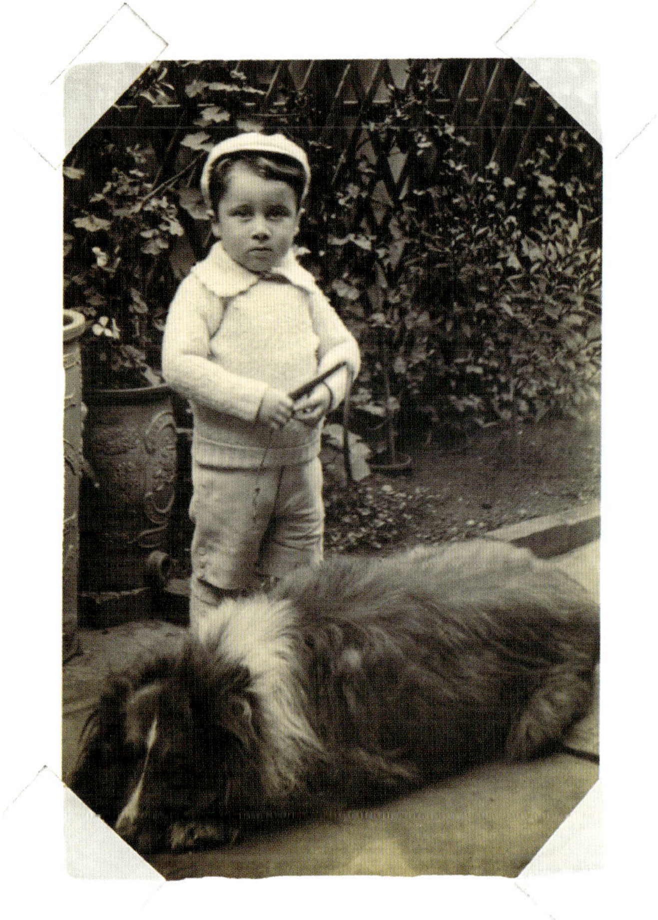

Some dogs are so faithful that they will never quit a thing entrusted to their charge, and will defend it to the utmost of their power.

*Anecdotes of Dogs by Edward Jesse, 1846*

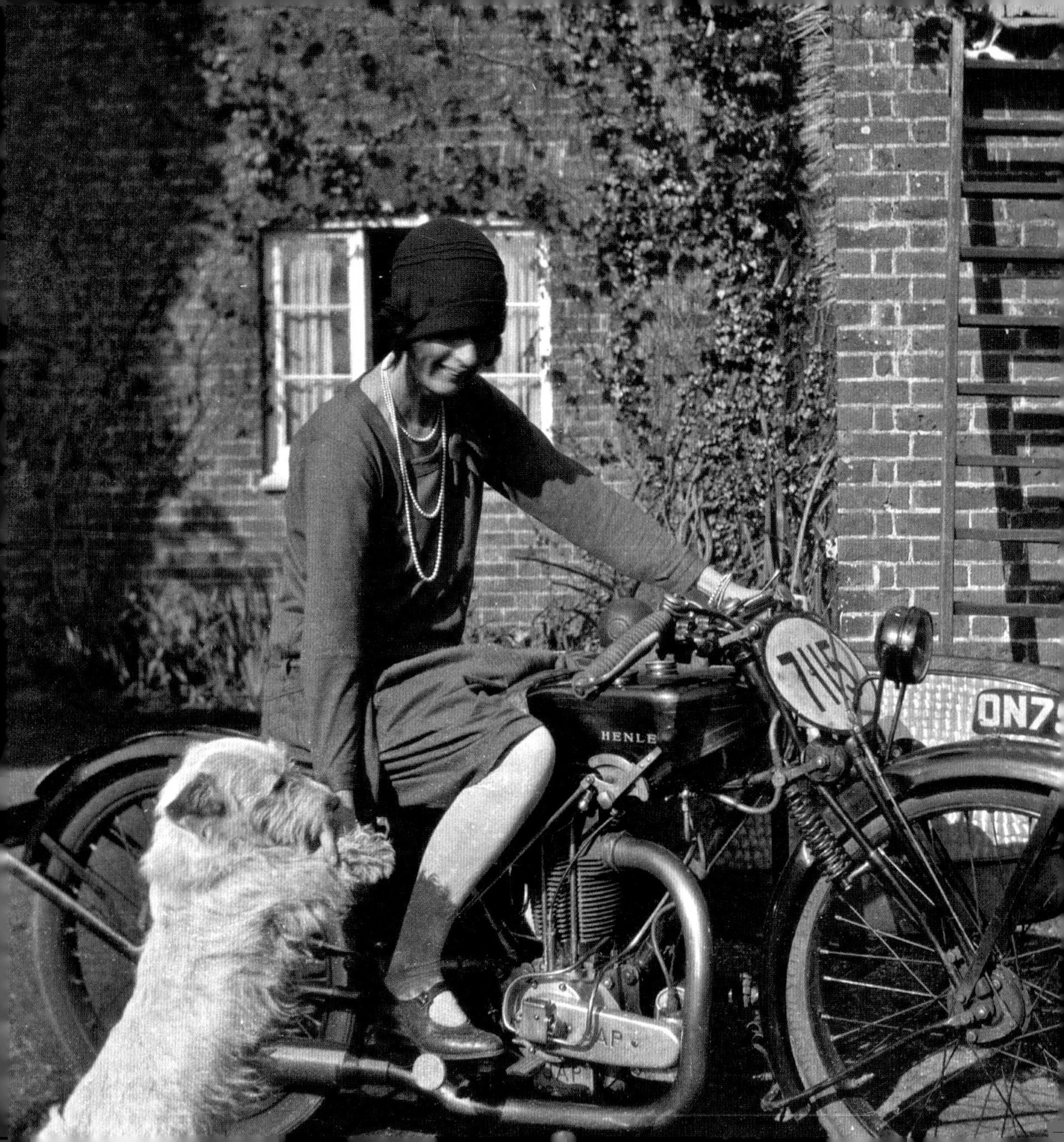
HENLE
ON7

How often does one find a truer fidelity to duty in the dog than in some human beings!

*Lieut.-Col. Edwin Hautenville Richardson, author*

Dogs are miracles with paws.

*Attributed to Susan Ariel Rainbow Kennedy, author and illustrator*

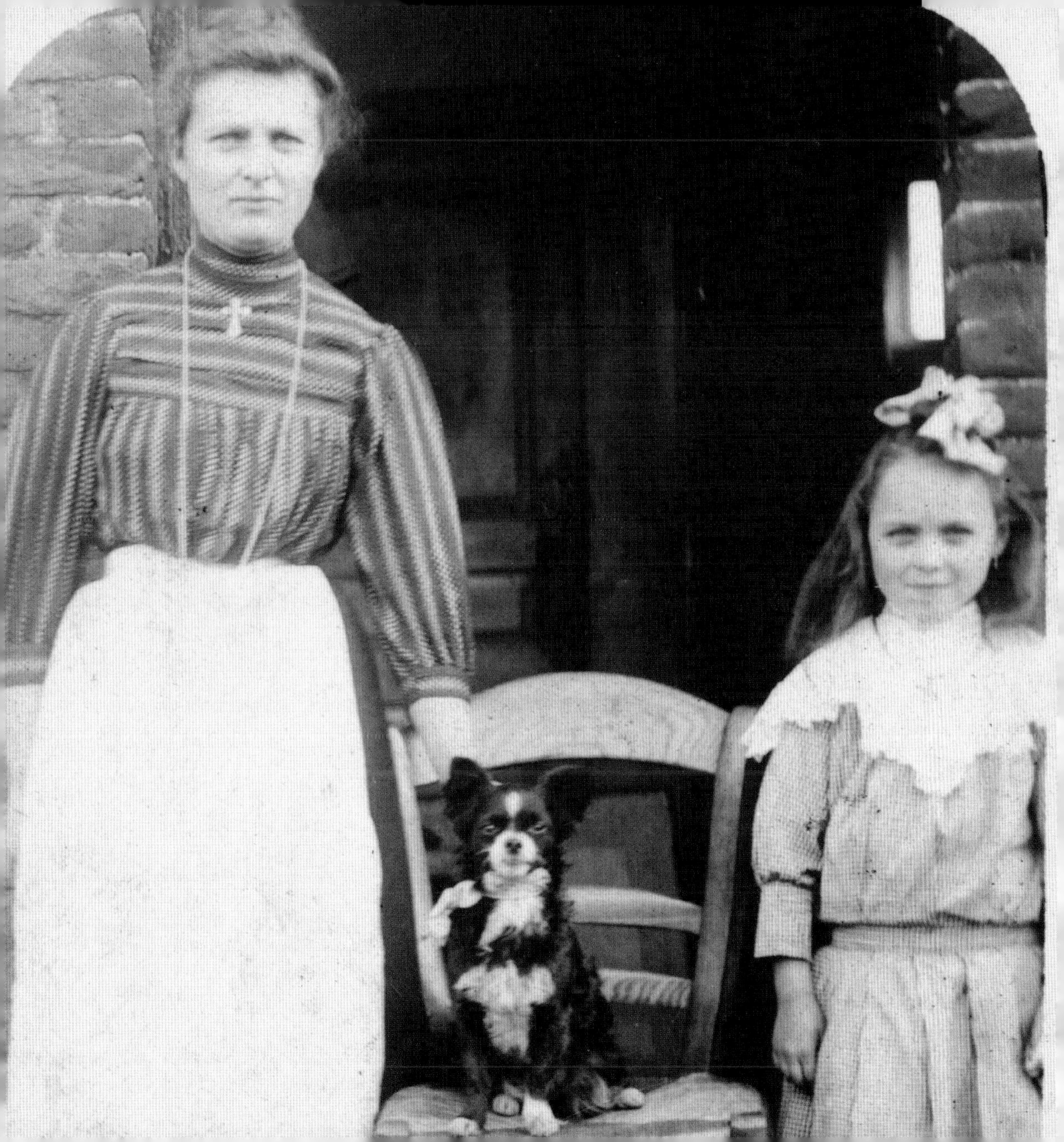

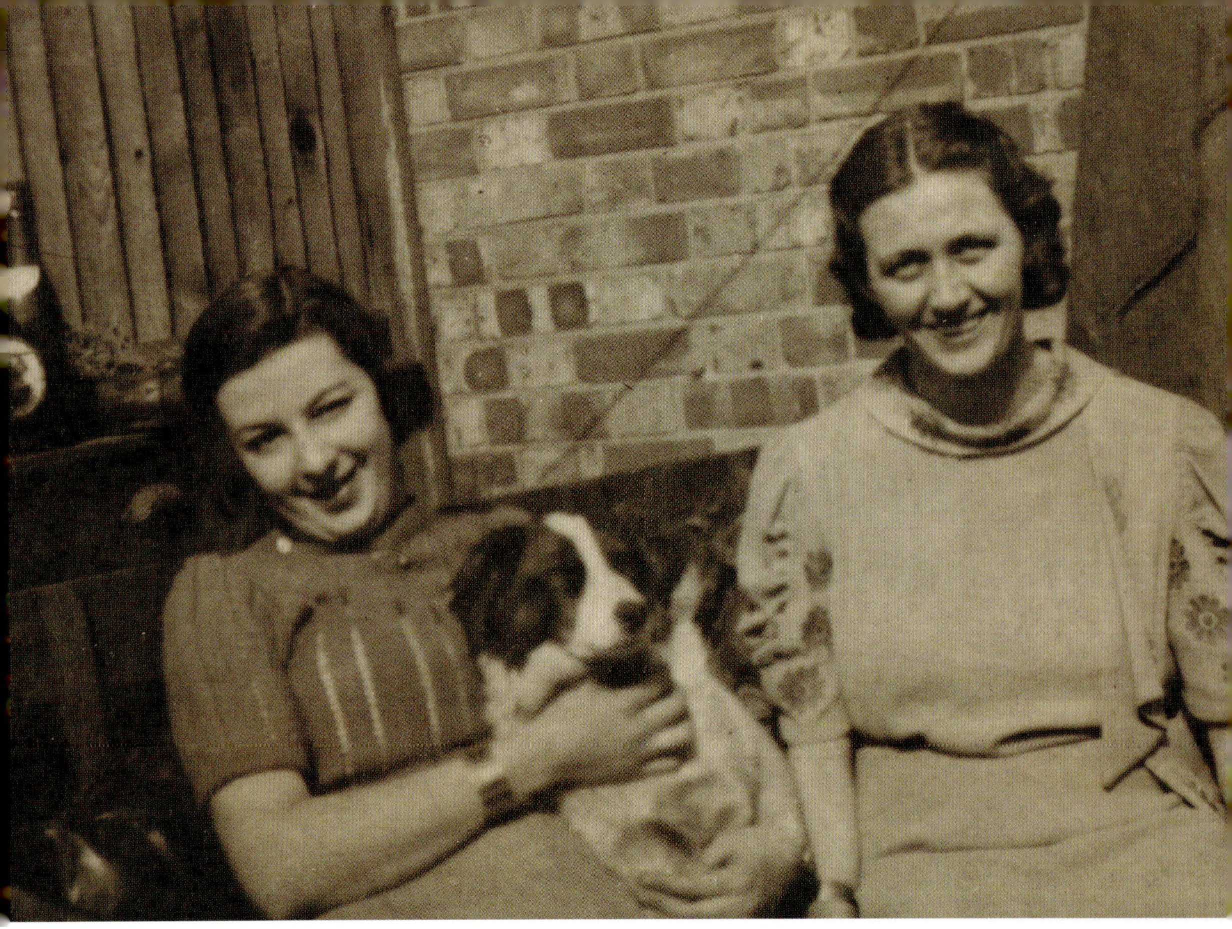

Scratch a dog and you'll find a permanent job.

*Franklin P. Jones, reporter*

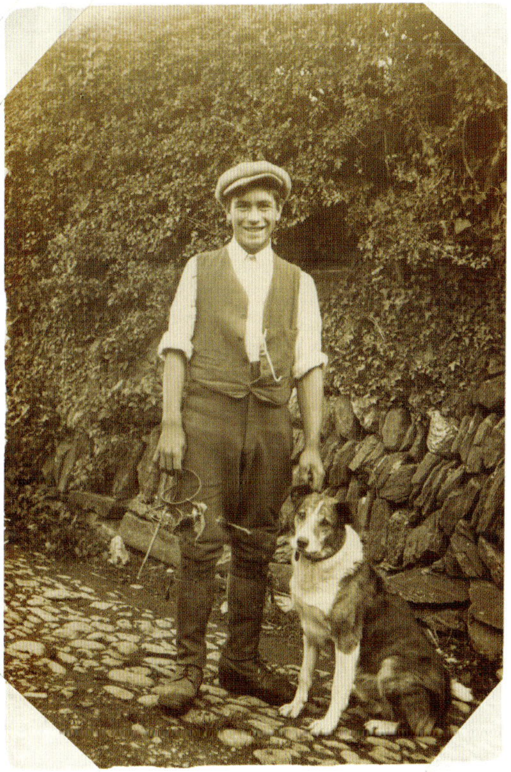

With eye upraised his master's looks to scan,
The joy, the solace, and the aid of man;
The rich man's guardian, and the poor man's friend,
The only creature faithful to the end.

*George Crabbe,*
*poet and clergyman*

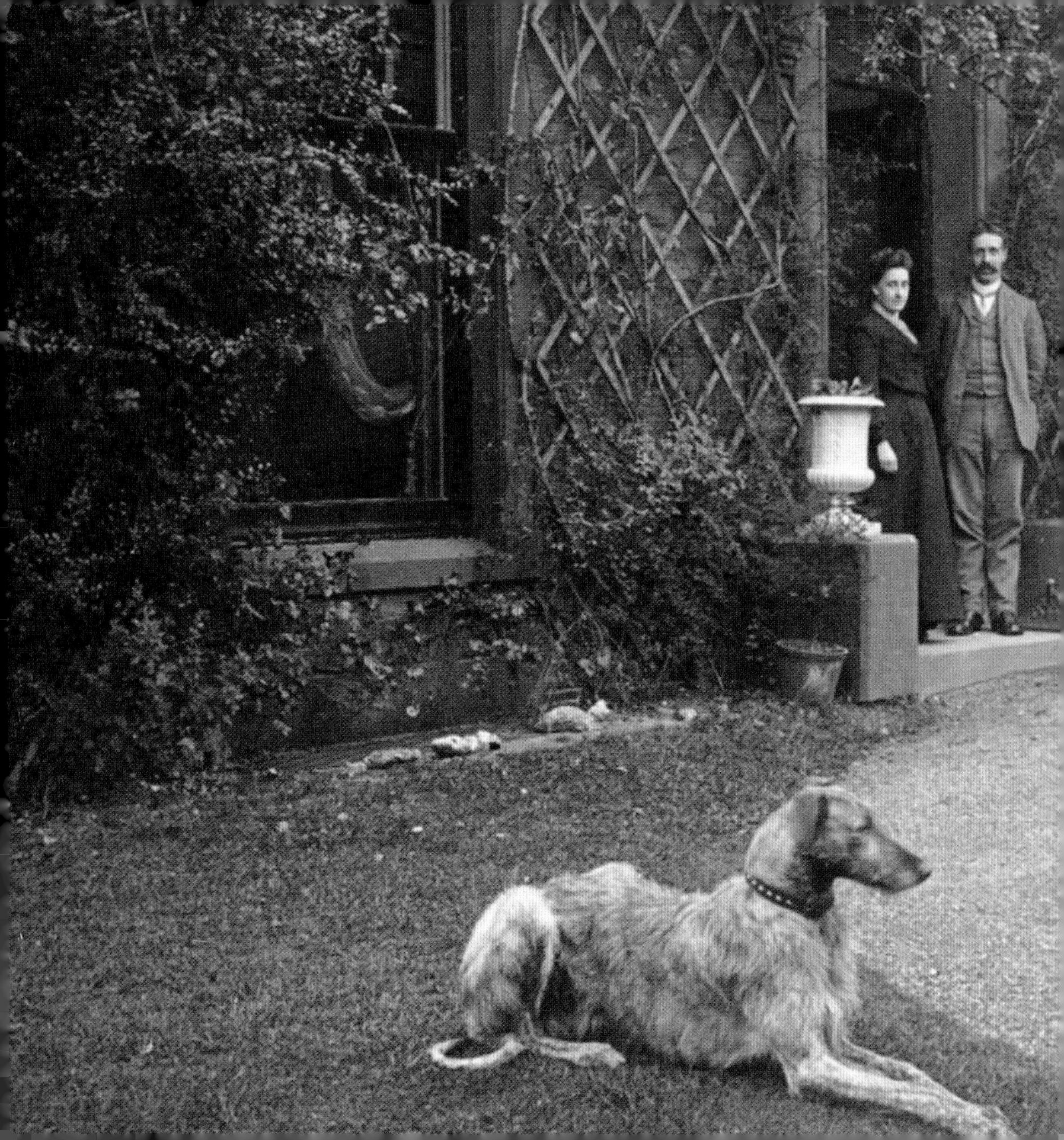